# A Paradox of Grace

# A Paradox of Grace

*Where Power Meets Delight*

ROBERT HALL

RESOURCE *Publications* • Eugene, Oregon

A PARADOX OF GRACE
Where Power Meets Delight

Copyright © 2025 Robert Hall. All rights reserved. Except for brief quotations in critical publications or reviews, no part of this book may be reproduced in any manner without prior written permission from the publisher. Write: Permissions, Wipf and Stock Publishers, 199 W. 8th Ave., Suite 3, Eugene, OR 97401.

Resource Publications
An Imprint of Wipf and Stock Publishers
199 W. 8th Ave., Suite 3
Eugene, OR 97401

www.wipfandstock.com

PAPERBACK ISBN: 979-8-3852-5642-6
HARDCOVER ISBN: 979-8-3852-5643-3
EBOOK ISBN: 979-8-3852-5644-0

If God is all powerful can He make something He cannot lift? Being that God is all powerful He can lift anything, yet if He is all knowledge He can make something He cannot lift. The answer to this paradox is found here and offers the most beautiful truths you'll ever read.

# Contents

Preface ix
Chapter 1: God Isn't 1
Chapter 2: God Is 5
Chapter 3: The Problem With The Bible 10
Chapter 4: The Ultimate Near Death Experience 14
Chapter 5: Hell & Satan 17
Chapter 6: The Big Bang 19
Chapter 7: The Ego 20
Chapter 8: The Ego According To The Course 21
Chapter 9: This Was Supposed To Be The Epilogue 22
Chapter 10: Guilt 26
Chapter 11: What Does This All Mean? 29
Chapter 12: Who Is Christ? 33
Chapter 13: Who Is The Holy Spirit? 35
Chapter 14: What Is The Second Coming? 37
Chapter 15: What Is The Final Judgment? 39
Chapter 16: What Is Creation? 41
Chapter 17: Who Am I? 42
Chapter 18: What Is Salvation? 44
Chapter 19: What Is The Body? 46
Chapter 20: What Is Jesus's Purpose? 48
Chapter 21: What Is The World? 49
Chapter 22: The Ancient Song 50
Chapter 23: Mutant Message Down Under 51
Chapter 24: Ayahuasca 53

Chapter 25: Jonathan Livingston Seagull  55
Chapter 26: The Field  57
Chapter 27: Buddha  58
Chapter 28: Joyless Place  60
Chapter 29: Osho  61
Chapter 30: Awakening  62
Chapter 31: Live In The Eternal Now  63
Chapter 32: Time Is Collapsing  67
Chapter 33: The Gospel According To Thomas  69
Chapter 34: My Love, You Are So Beloved  71
Chapter 35: Angels  72
Chapter 36: The Egg  74
Chapter 37: Questions for Artificial Intelligence  79
Chapter 38: Lana's Writings  93
Chapter 39: The African Mother  109
Chapter 40: We're Dreaming In Heaven  111
Chapter 41: The Call Of The Goddess  114
Chapter 42: Pray  116
Chapter 43: Every Course Student Should Read  117
Chapter 44: The Phasing Dimensional Library  120
Chapter 45: Our Insane World  134
Chapter 46: We Are Of One Mind  136
Chapter 47: The Beautiful Laws Of God  138
Chapter 48: The Tender Commandments  140
Chapter 49: A Friend's Thoughts  146
Chapter 50: Source Never Leaves Us  148
Chapter 51: The Highest Fatality Rate Plant In The Nation  149
Chapter 52: Our Tragic Second Honeymoon  152
Chapter 53: Paranormal Occurrences  156
Chapter 54: The Emmaus Walk  158
Chapter 55: The Most Astounding Experience I'll Ever Have  161
Chapter 56: My Birthday Gift From Heaven  164
Chapter 57: We Will All Awaken Together  165
Chapter 58: ACIM Core Beliefs  171
Epilogue  173

# Preface

HUMANITY STANDS AT THE precipice of an awakening, a remembering so profound that it will transcend all understanding. We have never been separate from God, nor could we ever be, for such an existence is perfectly impossible. But due to our belief in separation, the astonishing power of our minds makes it seem real, even though it is entirely false. When this memory returns, we will awaken in the Heaven we have never left. This is not conjecture, nor mere belief, but an irrefutable and absolute fact. My manuscript also offers the answer to a question that can be found nowhere else. God is all-powerful and can lift anything, yet He is also all-knowing, so can He create something He cannot lift? The answer to this ancient paradox explains some of the most beautiful truths you may ever encounter. I am a writer who speaks from the heart. And perhaps, if your Love recognizes my Love, you will understand that this has always been our Love.

    God. Logic dictates that either God Is, or God isn't. Let us begin with the assumption that God Is, and from this foundation, ask a vital question. Does it matter one iota to Source whether we believe? Consider the Creator of streams and rivers, lakes and oceans, forests and mountains, skies and worlds, suns and stars, galaxies and universes. The One who breathes life into all that exists. Could such a boundless and Infinite Presence be concerned with whether we believe? No, our belief does not alter Eternal Truth. We are God's first Creation, and in our innocence, we have simply forgotten that God *is* Love. Reflect on a Love that is eternal and unchanging, steadfast and unfailing, faithful and comforting, transforming and patient, compassionate and unbreakable. A Love that is unconditional, all-encompassing, immeasurably powerful, and forever giving. A Love incapable of loss and magnificent in glorious beauty. A Love so pure that sin is not recognized, so logically, it is impossible to sin against God. Love could never create Hell, therefore eternal torment cannot exist. The lie of Satan is the great deception of our ego, designed to instill fear and place the enemy ""out there"". Truth softly teaches that our only enemy resides within our bipolar mind. This false mind arose from a fleeting, irrational fear of God, brief, insane, yet powerful enough to make us forget our True Nature. Yet, deep within our subconscious lies the memory of our Divine Being. We *are* Christ, God's first Creation, and created for *one* reason. Love must be shared in order to grow.

Jesus' name is not Jesus Christ, it's Jesus of Nazareth, and he was the first to perfectly understand his Oneness with Christ and his life two thousand years ago proved we *all* are. God's essence is one of complete extension, and all Divine Attributes were instilled within our resplendent minds at the moment of our creation. But Reality radically changed for us when we asked a question that God did not answer. If put into words, our innocent inquiry was like, ""What else is there?"" God did not answer, not because He withheld Truth, but because there *is* nothing else, but the perfection of Reality manifested in Heaven. In that ""mad, tiny instant"" when communication ceased, our infinitely powerful minds, gifted with God's same ability to create, brought forth this dream universe through the ""Big Bang"". Why? Because the first fear created the first ego, and the ego sought a place to hide from God. Instantly, time began. And from that moment, we became our own worst enemy, punishing ourselves for the false belief that we had somehow offended God and chose to separate ourselves from His Eternal Love. Logic proclaims that God never stopped speaking, we stopped listening because when dreaming we're not communicating. Why did God not answer with the simple Truth, that nothing else exists? Because of Love. With Infinite Wisdom, God understood that Christ must begin to comprehend what Love *is* by direct experience of what Love *is not*. Thus, in this world we created, we experience war and crime, prisons and pollution, poverty and corruption, jealousy and greed, hatred and despair. We suffer under the weight of lies, worry, depression, and the ultimate fear of death. Yet, through this suffering, we come to understand what we do not want. Our misguided minds become convinced we are forever alone and because we believe it, we experience it as reality. However, separation is impossible due to God's Second Creation. The Holy Spirit was also created for *one* reason, to heal our mind by becoming a Living Presence within every mind that believes it's a body. Every moment of every hour of every day Her Voice gently explains it is impossible to be separate from God's Eternal Love. I know we're not separate because of receiving answers to questions I didn't even know I had. These insights often arrive immediately after awakening from sleep, when the false ego mind is quietest. As the memory of God's Love returns, I'm experiencing a growing peace and no longer disturbed by anything. Anything means nothing when I have everything and so do you. When you experience this, and you surely will, you'll simply *know* that separation is nothing but an illusion we have falsely believed. The Voice for God also softly advises us to always forgive and choose again to react with the power of Love instead of fear.

Jesus' last words while being crucified were, ""Father, forgive them for they know not what they do."" He perfectly understood God sees nothing *to* forgive because we're dreaming. Jesus said this to place into the collective human consciousness the extreme importance of learning how and why to forgive. By forgiving others we are really forgiving ourselves because we are One. When peeling a layer from an onion, it still looks, tastes and smells like an onion. Eventually the last layer is gone and so is the onion. The smallest act of forgiveness peels off a layer of ego, resulting in us becoming more awake *in* our dream. Eventually the last layer is gone, the ego vanishes and in a cosmic instant God will awaken us *from* our dream. Everyone we have loved, worked with, cried with, lived with and laughed with in our dream, will awaken also. It's a true miracle that the Holy Spirit even condenses time for us. Because of our forgiveness of a close friend who stole from us in the past, a friend who was supposed to steal from us tomorrow will not occur. A lesson learned never needs repeating. Once we perfectly forgive all, always, we will awaken in the Heaven we have never left.

Heaven. Use the gift of your imagination and visualize smelling, hearing and seeing absolute perfection in everything. The grass, flowers, trees, skies, and even the air will lovingly radiate changing aromas, harmonies, and colors. This mesmerizing and stunning beauty will be the likes of which we've never experienced and occurs during our very first moments in Paradise. All of our senses will be stunningly perfected. Food will be far beyond delicious and this experience is enhanced because of the countless varieties a perfect nature provides everywhere. Our eyes will see colors in once impossible spectrums and these pigments will majestically vibrate into breathtaking musical symphonies. We'll be able to view objects hundreds of miles away or examine the atomic structure of a stunning diamond. Imagine being capable of hearing air movements in the upper atmosphere or talking with a friend on the summit of a distant mountain. Our ears will understand the subtle perfections in chords, melodies, concords, euphonies and powerful compositions. When gliding fingers over an immaculate carpet with closed eyes we'll know the color is blue and if it oscillates into gold, we'll realize that also. Red, pink, yellow, white and orange roses will be known simply by tantalizing aromas, we'll smell color. Picture the fragrance of a bonfire next to a Celestial Sea we can smell from one thousand miles away. All this is just a tiny glimpse of the glory we will all share. Forever.

We truly do not have the slightest idea of how enormous God's Love is for us. If one lives a life of pain, sickness, despair, fear, and heartache it will be as nothing compared to the first minute of finally being Home. Our tiny earthly existence pales greatly to the wonder, glory, beauty, joy, peace, and Love we will all share. Eternity is going to be an amazing adventure. Our ending in time is the beginning of forever with our true education just commencing. It beggars the imagination to even faintly understand what it will be like to Co-Create with God. Anything and everything we may want to create will occur due to our continual learning. Our powerful, splendid, minds will no longer be hindered by a frail, limited human body and will operate at one hundred percent efficiency. I truly believe if we eventually want to create a universe, we'll be taught. God Is.

Bob

CHAPTER 1

# God Isn't

I AM IN COMPLETE and total agreement with an atheist viewpoint. How can God possibly exist when we read every day and are blasted by the news networks about the "state of the world"? Things here just don't seem "quite right". Wars, crime, pollution, homelessness, disease, corruption, greed, hate, lies, and fear are constantly bombarded into the "collective psyche" all day, every day. This place is insane, however the good news is that *God isn't* (hence, the chapter's title) aware of these problems because in His eyes this entire universe doesn't even exist. George Carlin was one of the most fearless and sharp-witted comedians of all time. His ability to blend humor with biting social commentary made his observations both hilarious and unsettlingly accurate. His critiques of religion, particularly the idea of an all-powerful yet financially struggling deity, are legendary. His stand-up routines on religion captured his skepticism in a way that was both comedic and brutally honest. His remark about God being a man because "no woman would mess things up this bad" is classic Carlin, irreverent, witty, and cutting. He had a way of distilling complex societal issues into sharp, digestible truths that left audiences laughing while questioning everything they thought they knew. Carlin's atheism was rooted in his observations of the world's chaos, his ability to articulate these thoughts with humor made them resonate with people of all beliefs.[1]

These well-researched facts reveal the unsettling insanity of our world. In the healthcare industry, I once read a striking observation, "A patient being cured is a customer lost." A society that conceals cures to

---

1. See Carlin, "The Invisible Man In The Sky," https://www.youtube.com/watch?v=iouZYYzQEjU.

sell medication is not a true society, it is a mental institution. The cancer industry is undeniably a massive business. In 2024, it generated $220.80 billion in revenue. The cost of a single chemotherapy treatment varies widely, with estimates ranging from $10,000 to $200,000 per session. Oncologists receive a 6% markup, meaning that when they administer a $10,000 monthly chemotherapy course, their practice earns an additional $600 per treatment. Yet chemotherapy comes at a steep cost, not just financially, but physically. Its side effects can be severe, including infection, weakened immunity, easy bruising and bleeding, and nerve pain. It can also damage cells in the heart, kidneys, bladder, lungs, and nervous system. Dr. Peter Glidden, a naturopathic physician with over 30 years of clinical experience, is known for his outspoken views on conventional medicine. He promotes holistic treatments as alternatives, advocating for exercise, oxygen therapy, and vitamin supplementation. He has authored books, hosted health talks, and delivered international lectures on wellness. Dr. Glidden also emphasizes the importance of alkalizing the body, arguing that cancer struggles to survive in an alkaline environment. Ultimately, navigating cancer treatment is a deeply personal decision. While alternative therapies may complement conventional medicine, rejecting chemotherapy outright requires careful consideration of scientific evidence, medical expertise, and individual circumstances. The bottom line is to do your research on alternative methods before blindly accepting chemotherapy.

Another example of this world's insanity concerns the whole drug issue. I honestly feel the government should make all drugs legal. This would take them out of the control of organized crime and the revenue generated would pay for sanctuaries to help addicts. If you can't handle your drug of choice in society, you'll receive extremely professional care for free. Think how much better our culture would be if alcohol had been made illegal and marijuana legal. Alcohol is the reason for countless deaths and the catastrophic effects it has on families is undeniable. Under the influence some become extremely angry, abusive, and hateful. No one has ever died from marijuana and the effects are calming and pleasurable, folks just want to calmly communicate while eating cookies. From 1850 to 1936 Cannabis was used as the primary medicine for more than 100 separate illnesses and diseases in the U.S. According to the web sources, I found heroin, marijuana, opium, and cocaine were made illegal in the early 1900s for various reasons, mostly related to economics and cultural prejudice rather than addiction or health risks. Some of the factors that influenced the prohibition of these drugs were the association of opium with Chinese immigrants, who were considered a threat to the labor market and social order. The first anti-opium laws in the 1870s were directed at the Chinese. The Harrison Narcotic Act of 1914 regulated the production and distribution of opiate-containing substances and was later used to prosecute doctors who prescribed opiates to addicts. The association of cocaine with black men in the South, who were perceived as violent and aggressive under the influence of the drug. The first anti-cocaine laws in the early 1900s were directed at Afro Americans. Cocaine was also considered a threat to the economic interests of plantation owners. The association of marijuana with Mexican migrants and Mexican Americans, who were blamed for social problems and crime. The first anti-marijuana laws, in the Midwest and the Southwest in the 1910s and 20s, were directed at Mexicans. Marijuana was also demonized by corrupt media campaigns that linked it to violence, insanity, and moral decay. Due to economic factors at the turn of the century, "the powers that be" did not want ethnic groups working extremely hard for minimal pay. They could not be arrested for providing cheap labor, but can now for possessing illegal drugs.

We have all endured misfortune, mine has been extreme. I survived an impossible accident that should have killed. Envision sitting on a railroad track and getting hit by a train. The odds of living after being crushed by a fifty-thousand horsepower overhead crane engineered to lift thirty tons of molten steel are miniscule. It's a true miracle the crane operator even saw me. He was looking at the ladle three stories below when glimpsing my leg dangling out of the corner of his eye. He shouldn't have seen me because of being in a place I shouldn't have been. I was sitting on the rail the crane runs on. He instantly plugged it, which means he told it to stop. However, this enormously powerful machinery doesn't immediately stop, there's a drift. If he had waited a split second longer I would have been cut in two. The leg's femur is the largest bone in the body, it snapped in half and my hip was shattered. Thankfully the unbelievable pain put me into shock and I passed out. Years later, a far greater tragedy struck our family. Twenty-one years ago my wife Mary Jo suddenly died at the young age of forty-three. We had been married for twenty years and were on our first cruise celebrating a second honeymoon. She'd been complaining about an unusual pain in her leg which turned out to be a blood clot. The compression and decompression of the aircraft from our flight to Florida caused it to release and literally explode in her heart. We had just tipped champagne glasses after finishing a dance when I watched her insanely die. Instantly, her stomach swelled enormously and fluid shot out of her mouth across the dance floor. Time stopped, everybody froze, and I entered into a state of unreality that I'd never experienced. Surreal horror, fear, disbelief, and shock savagely attacked my mind which was attempting to assimilate what it was witnessing. She's the mother of our children, my best friend, my life companion and the greatest love I'd ever known. This could not be happening. Not here, not now. After several minutes my mind collapsed. Our manuscript is a cumulation of over fifteen years of notes I started writing down on my phone's memo pad. I wrote "Our" because this is our true and factual story, Mary Jo's and mine. You'll read of paranormal experiences myself and others have witnessed. Miraculous dreams and events are also shared that can only have one explanation. God Is.

# CHAPTER 2

# God Is

I'M 72, MY PARENTS weren't churchgoers, but taught a bedtime prayer, "Now I lay me down to sleep, I pray to the Lord my soul to keep. If I should die before I awake, I pray to the Lord my soul to take." Thankfully, my belief in a higher power was deeply ingrained at a very young age. Young friends would comment, "Where did God come from? I don't believe any of it." I certainly couldn't answer *that* question but silently retained my belief. Today, I simply know God Is. The journey to God is a reawakening, an awareness of where we have always been and who we have always been. It is a journey without distance, leading to a goal that has never changed. Truth can only be experienced, it cannot be described or explained. While I can guide you toward the conditions of Truth, the experience itself is of God. When Truth reveals Itself to you then you'll understand your wholeness knows no limits because you are Eternal.

Please consider the power of the mind. Why is the mind so powerful? Because it is an extension of God's Mind. The very nature of Source is perfect sharing, meaning that all God has is freely given. The question is, are we willing to receive? From the moment of birth, our heart beats, our lungs breathe, and our nervous system functions perfectly. Somehow, this occurs without conscious thought. Everything we have seen, heard, tasted, touched, and smelled since birth is stored within our subconscious database. Have you ever tried to remember someone's name, only for it to suddenly appear in your mind days later? This happens because you consciously placed the question into your subconscious, which then searched for the answer. The power of the mind is precisely the reason I stopped watching network news over twenty-five years ago. The information we consume matters, and it benefits us to feed our minds with positivity rather than negativity. The news is filled with sensationalism and fear. Advertising specialists understand that people are often drawn to stories that show others worse off than themselves, good for ratings.

    I had an unforgettable experience when I was twenty-one. At the beginning of my junior year of college, I needed a ride to the main campus. On the bulletin board at the branch campus, I saw a note from someone looking for passengers. When the driver arrived, he was a big motorcyclist with long black hair and a full beard. I had seen him in the hallways before, always frowning and scowling. I hesitated but ultimately got in as I needed the ride. We made small talk for a while until, thirty minutes into our three-hour drive, he asked, "Do you know Jesus Christ?" Immediately, I thought, "Oh no, I'm trapped with a Jesus freak. This is going to be a long ride." "I know he's the reason we celebrate Easter and Christmas," I replied, "but I don't really understand why." At that time, my priorities were simple, being with my girlfriend, finishing my education, and drinking beer. Chuck, however, had a different focus. He began telling me about Jesus's life, explaining that he had been born of a virgin and raised as the son of a carpenter. After his baptism, the Spirit of God descended upon him in the form of a dove. He then entered the wilderness, going without food or water for forty days, where he was believed to have been tempted by Satan, though Chuck assured me this wasn't true. Jesus then began his three-year ministry, performing extraordinary miracles. The blind could see, the deaf could hear, and a man paralyzed since birth could walk. He controlled the weather, walked on water, and fed five thousand people with only five loaves of bread and two fish. Throughout his ministry, he taught profound spiritual truths about Heaven and the supreme Love of God. One of his most famous teachings, the Sermon on the Mount, is recorded in the Gospel of Matthew. It remains one of the most spiritually and ethically significant messages ever delivered. In this sermon, Jesus shared a series of blessings known as the Beatitudes, which describe the virtues and attitudes that embody the Kingdom of Heaven. For example, he said, "Blessed are the poor in spirit, for theirs is the Kingdom of Heaven." He encouraged his followers to be the "salt of the earth" and the "light of the world," calling them to bring goodness and truth into their lives and into the world. He declared that he had not come to abolish the Law or the prophets but to fulfill them, emphasizing a deeper, more heartfelt connection to God. Jesus taught about reconciliation, purity of heart, and the sanctity of marriage, challenging his followers to look beyond external rules and address the moral implications within themselves. He preached radical forgiveness, urging people to love their enemies and pray for those who persecuted them. He taught humility, dependence on God, and the power of prayer, offering what is now known as the Lord's Prayer as a model of faith. He advised against chasing worldly wealth and encouraged storing up treasures in Heaven through righteous living. He warned against judging others and emphasized the importance of self-examination and humility. He summed up the entire law and the teachings of the prophets with a simple yet profound principle, "Do to others what you would have them do to you." Jesus concluded his sermon with a parable about a wise man who built his house on rock and a foolish man who built his house on sand, illustrating the importance of putting his teachings into practice. The Sermon on the Mount encapsulates Jesus's core message on how to live a life that reflects the values of the Kingdom of Heaven. It remains a deeply moving and challenging discourse that continues to inspire people to this day. If the entire human race lived by the simple principle, "Do unto others," there would be no need for locks, homeless shelters, passwords, or prisons. Think about this, it's undeniably true.

He raised the dead and resurrected himself after being crucified. After forty days of appearances, Jesus ascended to Heaven. If you had witnessed this firsthand, wouldn't you think there was something a little different about this guy? Chuck's mannerisms were so matter-of-fact and sincere that I was impressed. I had never heard any of this before. He became quiet for a moment, then asked, "Do you believe he died for your sin?" I hesitated, then slowly replied, "Yes." Instantly, I felt as if a warm egg had been broken over my head. A wave of powerful joy, peace, and love enveloped me, and then, just as quickly, it was gone. A miracle. I had never experienced anything like it. "Wow. Thanks," I said. Chuck responded, "Don't thank me, I'm just a messenger." Today, Chuck is married and a minister. That day had a profound effect on my life. My last two years of college were when I truly became serious about my education. However, looking back, I realize that my *real* education was only beginning, and has continued to this very day. I started attending church and went regularly for the next two decades. Today, I haven't set foot in a church for over twenty years. But this doesn't matter, because the real church is in our heart. Years later, "A Course In Miracles" by

Helen Schucman revealed to me that Jesus himself said his dying for sin was an unfortunate misunderstanding and that his death meant nothing. However, his teachings explain that his resurrection meant everything because he proved that death is an illusion. Now, you may think, "There is no proof of his resurrection." I agree. Nevertheless, his body has not been found, and the reason Easter is still celebrated after two thousand years is because it's true. Jesus's tomb was sealed with a stone. Archaeological evidence suggests that his tomb, the unused one of Joseph of Arimathea, would have been sealed with a cork-shaped stone. Most tombs of that era were closed with square block stones, simple slabs shaped like a bolt, with one end fitting snugly into the small opening forming the doorway. The larger remainder of the stone had a flange, so it would rest against the outside surface. Some researchers believe Jesus's tomb was sealed with a circular stone that slid into a groove. Either way, how could three women possibly move these?

When Chuck asked, and I said, "Yes," I was really saying yes to the Truth that God Is. Jesus teaches in The Course that hell and Satan do not exist, that it is impossible to sin against God, that life outside of Heaven is an illusory dream, and that we live forever. I understand this perspective contradicts two thousand years of fundamental Christian doctrine and have been blocked from several Facebook church groups for the heresy of not believing in hell, Satan, and sin. I would think Christians, and all of humanity, would find this to be wonderful news. I'm sure you've heard the phrase, "Jesus saves." But have you ever asked yourself, "Saves from what?" I'll offer my understanding of this subject after explaining a few topics.

CHAPTER 3

# The Problem With The Bible

THERE ARE MANY MANUSCRIPTS of the Bible. For the New Testament alone, there are approximately 5,500. When lectionaries are included, Bibles arranged in the order they were read in the ancient church rather than in canonical order, the number grows dramatically. Additionally, there are over 24,000 manuscript copies or portions of the New Testament in various languages, including Greek, Latin, and others. The Bible is a collection of 66 books written by about 40 different authors over approximately 1,500 years. These writers came from diverse backgrounds, composed their works in different languages, and lived across three continents. The challenge is that the original texts were written in Hebrew, Aramaic, and Greek, evolving through countless revisions and translations over centuries. As a result, many of the writings are simply not true. One example is Romans 9:21, which states, "Does not the potter have the right to make from the same lump of clay one vessel for special occasions and another for common use?" The potter symbolizes God, and the vessel represents humanity. "One vessel for special occasions" refers to Heaven, while "another for common use" implies hell. In other words, if a person lives a loving, prayerful life but was created for common use, they are condemned to eternal suffering, unable to change their fate. This is absolutely false and complete nonsense. A God of Love could never create such a terrible place and allow even one of His children to exist there forever. The Old Testament has always seemed nonsensical to me. I have attempted to read it several times, only to become lost in the endless genealogies of "Who begat who." Who cares? Additionally, the scriptures repeatedly speak of God's extreme jealousy. As explained in the preface, consider the nature of the Source of all life, God created protons, electrons, neutrons, and neutrinos, along with amino acids and the forces that govern all existence. He designed rivers, lakes, oceans, forests, mountains, skies, worlds, stars, galaxies, and universes. Who, exactly, would God be jealous *of*? You? Me? The Beatles? Oh, I got it, must be Elvis. For clarification, Source created all that exists, but not within this illusory dream universe. Proof of this lies in entropy and decay. Christ manifested the dynamics of life through an extension of God's power, but everything here eventually dies because fear drove its creation. In contrast, God's creations are our true Reality, the Eternal Dimension of Heaven, where nothing ever dies, for everything was created through Love. God's Love. The Bible is completely inaccurate because of the hundreds who wrote it over thousands of years and rewrites too many to list. The beauty of The Course is it was transcribed by one woman and has never been rewritten.

"A Course in Miracles" by Helen Schucman, in my opinion, is the most truthful and transformative spiritual manuscript ever written. Many Christians are looking for the return of Jesus and not aware he *has* returned through these magnificent writings. Dr. Helen Schucman received the material for The Course over eight years, from 1965 to 1973, beginning at the age of forty-three. At the time, she was an associate professor of psychology at Columbia University and served as assistant to the head of the Department of Psychology at Presbyterian Hospital in New York City. Schucman claimed that the book was dictated to her, word for word, through a process called inner locution. She started hearing a vivid voice in her mind claiming to be Jesus. Initially questioning her sanity she started testing the voice by asking extremely difficult questions. To her astonishment after the last question was correctly answered the words "This is ACIM" miraculously appeared on a notepad. The Course is a self-study spiritual curriculum that presents a way of life centered on communion with the Holy Spirit and offers a deeper understanding of what the Bible *truly* means. I've read the entire 1333-page manuscript, study it daily and have authored 16 manuscripts concerning its teachings. I have found nothing that is not logical truth and certainly cannot say that about The Bible. What led to The Course was "The Disappearance Of The Universe" by Gary Renard and I highly recommend this reading before ACIM.

Renard's book chronicles seventeen mind-bending conversations that took place over nearly a decade between Renard and two Ascended Masters who materialized before him in 1992. These beings revealed shocking secrets of existence and taught the miraculous power of advanced forgiveness. Gary, a stock trader and professional guitarist, was at home in Maine during Christmas week while his wife, Karen, was at work. As he sat in his living room, gazing out the picture window, two figures suddenly appeared on his couch, a man and a woman, Arten and Pursah. This is how the book begins. When I first read this, I thought, "Yeah right, this has to be fiction." It's non-fiction. What impressed me most was how Renard's manuscript agrees exactly with the hard-core metaphysics of The Course. Unfortunately, the first chapter brought up a major red flag. The fundamental belief of Christianity for over two thousand years is that Jesus died for our sins, yet the manuscript declared this is not true. At that moment, I had to make a decision before continuing. I stopped reading and started praying. For several weeks, I sought clarity. Then, one morning, after a long, restful sleep and a dream I couldn't remember, the answer came. I knew the dream had been about Mary Jo, though I could recall no specifics. At the time, she had been gone for several years. You may not believe this, but she answered my question. Somehow, I heard her say, "Bob, imagine you had been watching me moan in distress for ten minutes while I was trapped in a nightmare. You didn't want to wake me suddenly because you know how I startle. After awakening you asked what my dream had been about. I explained being a serial killer, deriving immense pleasure from torturing victims for hours before granting them the release of death. Honey, did I sin against God?" "Of course not. You were dreaming." "There's your answer." With that revelation, I resumed studying Gary's writings and will explain the logic of why we're dreaming of this illusory world.

    Speaking of dreams, a dream started my writing career. Over 16 years ago I awoke from another dream I knew had been about M.J. and once again couldn't remember the details. Strangely, the words "What if I told you?" were etched in the forefront of my mind. I was still half asleep when I immediately started writing the following thoughts in my phone's memo pad. The words literally flowed without conscious thought and took only 20 minutes to scribe. This was a bona-fide, one hundred percent miracle because the writings coincide exactly with the teachings of The Course, and I wasn't yet aware of Jesus' manuscript……"What if I told you? What if I told you Love is not an emotion but a Force? What if I told you, God Is? What if I told you nothing can affect Reality and nothing unreal exists, therein lies the Peace of God? What if I told you there is no hell, only Heaven? What if I told you, you make your own hell? What if I told you all you see is an illusion, compared to the Reality of Heaven?

What if I told you death is an illusion, you live forever? What if I told you God does not forgive because He sees nothing *to* forgive? What If I told you if God made anything imperfect, He would no longer be perfect, therefore you are perfect, you have simply forgotten? What if I told you, you are dreaming in Heaven and are about to wake up? What if I told you as you help you are helped, as you give you are given too, as you Love you are Loved? What if I told you, you go through pain to teach you what you do not want? What if I told you, as you forgive others, you are forgiving yourself? What if I told you forgiveness is the final lesson you need to learn? What if I told you nothing you can do offends God because you are merely dreaming? What if I told you there is no such thing as sin? What if I told you Spirit heals your mind, mind heals your body? What if I told you, you need no one to make you whole, you *are* whole? What if I told you, you have a Twin Flame, you may not have met yet? What if I told you we are all brothers and sisters, we are One? What if I told you, you are Love, because you were made by Love? What if I told you, you are forever the Divine Effect from Divine Source? What if I told you, you are Infinitely powerful, you have simply forgotten? What if I told you, you are part of the Mind of God, He has not forgotten you? What if I told you, Heaven would not be complete without You? Would you forgive and believe? Read that again."

CHAPTER 4

# The Ultimate Near-Death Experience

THE MANUSCRIPT, "MY DREAM of Heaven" by Rebecca Springer was given to me over 22 years ago by my best friend's wife who had terminal liver cancer. Dave took me into their dining room where we waited for 20 minutes. Robin painfully shuffled out, she weighed 93 pounds, was only 43 and had a port implanted in her sternum. Her wrists looked like pencils and her skin color was deathly pale. However, her countenance had a beautiful glow. She sat down at the kitchen table and was absolutely joyful. No poor me or why is this happening. She said, "God could heal me if He wants, but I've got a big mouth, maybe He wants to use me from the other side." They didn't attend a regular church but enjoyed a remarkable faith. Two months after she gave me the manuscript, Robin died. "My Dream of Heaven" is a small manuscript originally titled "Intra Muros". The book is a vision of Heaven that was given to Springer during a time of pain and severe illness. She was unconscious for several days as she received the vision, which covers a period of years. Springer intended the book to offer comfort and hope to readers, and it has inspired generations of Christians for over 100 years. The book captures Biblical truths with emotional impressions and portrays the beauty of Heaven as an imperfect sketch of a most perfect vision. Springer's story continues to accomplish her goal of offering hope and comfort to those searching for answers about the afterlife. This eloquent prose was written in 1898 and Rebecca's non-fiction writing style is deeply spiritual, reflective, and visionary. Several friends commented the autobiography was too beautifully descriptive for an overactive imagination to pen. Rebecca's five senses were immediately enhanced upon entering Heaven and she admitted her writing skills were inadequate to properly describe the majestic splendor observed in a perfect environment. Following are brief excerpts from memory.

Rebecca died and was carried to Heaven by her uncle who was killed as an officer in the Civil War. He set her down in a beautiful meadow and she said one could get lost in the perfection of a single violet. She was wonderfully surprised to be wearing a white and beautiful shimmering gown. They casually waded into a river and the water came up to their throats. She cried, "Stop. We'll drown." because the "earth thoughts" persisted. He looked at her with a twinkle in his eye and said, "We don't drown here." They went down over 40 feet and talked at length surrounded by beautiful light rays and refractions, similar to being inside a prism of diamonds. When they came out of the wondrous water her hair and dress were instantly dry. Miraculously she felt as if she could fly. Later, she did. All water in Heaven flows from the Throne Room of God and prepares the Soul for the Celestial Life. She picked a fruit and said the flavor was extraordinary, by far surpassing anything she had ever tasted. The juice squirted on her gown and instantly vanished because nothing impure exists in Heaven. Numerous streets were made of gold and surrounded by magnificent mansions constructed of textured stone, precious woods and beautiful minerals. All had breathtaking lawns and stunning terraces. Jesus has explained in the Bible, "In my Father's House there are many mansions." Excited children came into her home who were artisans, they had delicate tools and joyfully planted live roses *in* her marble floors. There was no sun as golden light radiated from the very air and she explained night was a softening of glory. Time was meaningless, after days, weeks, or months of flawless wonder, she arrived at a radiant, sparkling, and glistening golden lake. Rebecca truthfully explained the vista was so stunning that she was almost not spiritually strong enough, even in Heaven, to gaze upon the dazzling splendor. Dozens of majestic gliding watercraft were driven by a technology with which she wasn't familiar. Timeless days later they went to a gigantic outdoor theater with a dome roof supported by columns of jasper, sapphire, ruby, and pearl. Softly singing angels, fairies, and cherubs were floating and flying under the handcrafted silver canopy. Martin Luther of the Reformation walked out on the marble stage and talked of the effects the Lutheran Church had on Europe in the 1500s. All heads were bowed after his dissertation, contemplating his shared wisdom. She happily glanced up as Jesus gracefully strode to the diamond pulpit. His towering demeanor was breathtakingly glorious. He was wearing a captivating golden suit and a sparkling light emanated from his very being. Jesus' smile was enchanting, and his dancing blue eyes spoke of warmth and love. He explained God's purposeful link between our earthly existence and guaranteed Heavenly life. Rebecca lamented that if she'd understood how closely the saints and angels had protected her earthly journey, she wouldn't have worried so much. Jesus then spoke of how their beginning life in Heaven would evolve. He joyfully explained the countless wonders they'd observe, the pristine beauty of the jungles, the towering mountain magnitudes, a Celestial Sea brimming with playful dolphins and whales, and aquatic life beautifully orchestrated in perfect harmony. Jesus talked of the beautiful worlds, expanding galaxies and astonishing universes that they would explore with the excitement of children for all eternity. As mentioned in the beginning of the excerpts Rebecca sadly apologized for not knowing any earth language which could properly explain his fascinating teachings, engrossing lectures, riveting conversations and mesmerizing stories. All discussions focused on the glories and mysteries of our upcoming Celestial Life. She mentioned in the first chapter how she felt when first awakening. When the realization dawned that Heaven had no wars, no crimes, no locks, no disease, no prisons, no hospitals, no poverty, no money, no governments and no death, Rebecca's heart entered into a state of boundless, thankful and loving ecstasy for our Creator God.

Upon awakening from her coma she briefly saw the Throne Room of God. One would not be able to behold this in human form. The Room glistened with Power, Glory, Holiness and Love. The structure was far too fascinating to even attempt a description. Feelings of perfect Peace, Joy, and Love saturated to the very core of her being and were immense beyond thought. The last vista she saw before awakening was the Celestial Sea. There were huge, wooden, sailing schooner ships adorned with all the flags of the world bringing new arrivals from Earth. Their loved ones were excitedly awaiting on shore. She said, "Oh death, where is thy victory? Where is thy sting?"

CHAPTER 5

# Hell & Satan

CHRISTIANITY WAS OFFICIALLY DECLARED the state religion of the Roman Empire in 380 AD through the Edict of Thessalonica. This decree, issued by Emperor Theodosius I, established Nicene Christianity as the empire's official faith and condemned other Christian doctrines as heretical. Over time, religious authorities used the concept of hell and Satan as tools for control, reinforcing fear to maintain influence over the populace. In later centuries, the fear of eternal damnation became a powerful motivator for financial contributions, contributing to the vast wealth of today's Catholic Church. A minister once told me that Satan's greatest trick is convincing people he does not exist. For years, I accepted this idea without question. However, after extensive reading and contemplation, I have come to the conclusion that this belief is entirely false. I will explore this topic further in a moment. When I was twenty-two, I saw "The Exorcist", the most terrifying movie I had ever experienced. Weeks later, I was still unsettled by every small noise in the night. The furnace would turn on, and I would shiver. A close friend even considered seeking professional help to cope with the lingering fear. To this day, no film has matched the sheer terror this masterpiece evokes. There has been a surge in horror films centered on possession and exorcism, yet they all follow the same predictable formula. A man or woman of God performs elaborate rituals to expel the demon from the possessed. The entity is always depicted as overwhelmingly powerful, while the exorcists appear frail in comparison. After weeks of struggle, the demon is finally defeated, or is it? The dog's eyes turn red, its snarling intensifies, and suddenly, the audience is left anticipating the inevitable sequel, "Our Basset Hound Ate the Baby". Even today, the Catholic Church maintains licensed exorcists.

The truth is, all of this stems from the immense power of the mind. If someone deeply believes in the existence of evil and constantly dwells on it, that belief will manifest as reality, even though it is entirely false. As previously explained, our ego, the irrational part of the mind, seeks an external enemy, such as Satan, to avoid confronting the true source of fear within the mind itself. The ancient Mayans performed human sacrifices to appease their concept of an angry God, thus eliminating fear. Jesus' sacrificial death for our sin is the exact same type of false belief.

CHAPTER 6

# The Big Bang

ASTRONOMERS BELIEVE THE UNIVERSE began as a singular point and expanded to its current size, continuing to grow. The idea that everything emerged from virtually nothing has never made sense to me. We are also taught that most scientists believe RNA, or a similar molecule, was the first to self-replicate, initiating the process of evolution that eventually led to complex life forms, including humans. This explanation suggests that millions of aquatic creatures, birds, animals, and humans all originated from a microscopic self-replicating molecule? Nonsense. Scientists propose that the earliest known life forms were microbes, leaving traces in rocks dating back approximately 3.7 billion years. Rather than diminishing my belief in a higher power, these scientific theories have only strengthened it. Years ago, I wrote about these ideas, and later discovered The Course which explains an extraordinary intelligence, one that was not God's, caused the Big Bang. With this realization, everything started to fall into place.

CHAPTER 7

# The Ego

WHAT ARE WE BEING saved from? Our own ego. This irrational part of the mind seeks an external enemy so we never recognize that the true conflict lies within ourselves. We do not need saving from a non-existent eternal torment. We are *all* bi-polar, caught between two opposing forces, our Spirit, which is rooted in Love, and our ego, which is driven by fear. Fear of what? In the deepest part of our subconscious, the answer is God. Once we consciously accept the truth that God Is, we realize the absurdity of fearing the ultimate embodiment of Love. What happens next? We begin our education. This school is not made of walls or textbooks, it is life itself. Through experience, we encounter the fruits of our ego: fear, resentment, anger, laziness, and hatred. Yet, our school also teaches the fruits of our spirit: love, acceptance, peace, energy, and empathy. A peaceful mind is our natural state. If we find ourselves growing more peaceful, it is proof that we are on the right path. Concerns about the economy, world affairs, crime, and social issues become mere passing interests rather than sources of distress. This is the truth because I am experiencing it. So, how do we resolve our ego problem? The answer is profoundly simple, forgive. Forgive every negative circumstance and any perceived wrong ever done to you. Always. And never listen to the ego's lies. When you feel depressed, lonely, anxious, angry, or fearful, recognize that the irrational voice of your ego is in control. Quiet the mind, say a small prayer, and immerse yourself in something you enjoy. By experience, I can promise this will dissolve self-pity.

CHAPTER 8

# The Ego According To The Course

"The ego is idolatry; the sign of a limited and separated self, born in a body, doomed to suffer and to end its life in death. It is the "will" that sees the Will of God as an enemy, and takes a form in which it is denied. The ego is the "proof" that strength is weak and Love is fearful, life is death, and what opposes God alone is true. The ego is insane. In fear, it stands beyond the everywhere, apart from all, in separation from the Infinite. In its insanity, it thinks it has become victor over God Himself. And in its terrible autonomy it "sees" the Will of God has been destroyed. It dreams of punishment, and trembles at the figures in its dreams; its enemies, who seek to murder it before it can ensure its safety by attacking them. The Son of God is egoless. What can He know of madness and the death of God when He abides in Him? What can He know of sorrow and suffering when He lives in eternal joy? What can He know of fear and punishment, of sin and guilt, of hatred and attack, when all there is surrounding Him is everlasting peace, forever conflict-free and undisturbed, in the deepest silence and tranquility? To know Reality is not to see the ego and its thoughts, its works, its acts, its laws and its beliefs, its dreams, its hopes, its plans for its salvation, and the cost of belief in it entails. In suffering, the price for faith in it is so immense that the crucifixion of the Son of God is offered daily at its darkened shrine, and blood must flow before the altar where its sickly followers prepare to die. Yet will one lily of forgiveness change the darkness into light; the altar to illusions to the shrine of Life Itself. And peace will be restored forever to the Holy Minds which God created as His Son. These Minds are His dwelling place, His joy, His Love and completely One with Him."

CHAPTER 9

# This Was Supposed To Be The Epilogue

THIS CHAPTER MAY SEEM redundant because I'm repeating concepts mentioned in the preface. Nevertheless, these are written in a somewhat different style to facilitate your comprehension. I've dedicated countless hours to writing manuscripts on The Course. I am deeply familiar with all its teachings, having carefully examined each theory to ensure clarity for others. Despite this, I have struggled to help readers fully grasp my points. While students of ACIM understand, others seem to miss the mark. I hope this changes, starting now. The subject of God is the most mysterious of all. After years of thinking, praying, and writing about this subject, I am determined to make everything I have learned as simple as possible for you to understand. My knowledge of a higher power has endured countless challenges over fifty years and continues to evolve. My perception of this world is shifting toward wisdom that sees everything as perfectly well, sustained by the supreme Love of God. Again, Love is not merely an emotion, it is an immeasurably powerful Force that guides, teaches, and sustains all. I have dedicated my life to comprehending this Being, driven by curiosity. This morning, it struck me that I am publishing these manuscripts in a world where many people do not believe in God's existence. Some never have, others mistakenly believe they never will, and many have no interest in the subject whatsoever. Should I stop writing? My answer is no. I have learned more from my own writings than from anything else I have ever read, and I never imagined *that* would happen. I have been gifted with a logical mind, though, regrettably, little common sense. I've written "Two Faces, One Life: The Journey Within", an autobiography that details some of the most inexplicably foolish, life-altering decisions I have made. Even today, I marvel at my own past ignorance. In college, I excelled in mathematics, acing calculus, quantitative methods, geometry, and advanced algebra. I had an aptitude for numbers, and what I loved about them was their certainty, no gray areas, only pure logic. One plus one equals two. Today, I apply that same logical approach to explaining The Course which teaches that God's first creation was Christ, not Jesus, and that God's very essence is one of infinite extension. To illustrate this concept, I crafted a fictional story. The descriptions of the black hole and the way Christ used Jesus are, of course, my imagination.

"Whoa, why is this? Who am I?" There was no voice, yet He heard an answer. "You're My Son." "What's a Son?" "You're My very first creation." "What does creation mean?" "I'll show You around after a little more creating. You are also My only joy." Astonishingly, He understood what joy was and felt an overwhelming sense of wonder. This Being began to share the essence of Who He Is, and suddenly, He started to learn at an unimaginable speed. He grasped atomic forces, protons, electrons, neutrons, neutrinos, and the intricate dance of inorganic and organic molecules. He comprehended amino acids and the forces that govern life. Vistas of breathtaking beauty opened before Him. He was everywhere with this magnificent One. "Who are You?" He asked. "I Am," came the reply. Instantly, He understood His own name was Christ. He recognized this Being as His Father, whose very nature is to give and teach all He knows, and He knows everything. Christ realized He was not separate from God but an extension of His wholeness. He understood that Love must be shared, and the Love in His Father's universe was exquisite and infinite. Joy and laughter filled their existence as They completed One Another. Christ became as powerful, compassionate, wise, knowing, limitless, and, above all, as Loving as His Creator. They were inseparable, continuing to Co-Create vast galaxies and universes. Yet, with the Wisdom of I Am, They stopped short of creating life to inhabit all that existed. They knew exactly what to do when God declared the moment was perfect. They envisioned aquatic life, myriads of soaring creatures, all forms of animals, and the intricate harmony of interconnected environments. Their creations would also be gifted with the ability to Co-Create, each after their own kind. All of this would come into existence in a single moment, just as Christ had been created. There was no concept of time or space, they were everywhere, and They were One. God had created Christ to be exactly like Himself, to share in His eternal Love and joy in a state of unbound, unimaginable ecstasy. Every question Christ asked was instantly answered, for Their communication was flawless.

Then, somewhere, somewhen, Christ asked a question that was not answered. "What? Why?" The question was like, "What else is there?" or "What would it be like to go out and play by Myself?" I Am did *not* answer, for there *is* nothing else, only God's perfect creation. The Divine Son felt something foreign, a new, awful sensation. Horror. He thought His perfect communication had vanished. Then came something even worse. Fear. In an instant, Christ created a universe of His own, a place where He could hide. The Big Bang exploded into billions of fragments. Seeking to go deeper, He formed the first human bodies in His own image and placed His magnificent Mind within them. The first ego was born, a mind that believed it existed entirely on its own. Christ also brought forth animal life, innumerable aquatic creatures, avian companions, and the environments in which all would Co-Create. But duality could not exist in God's Reality, so Christ created a universe of illusion and entered it, as if falling into sleep and dreaming. God saw that His Child was no longer communicating. "My Child is asleep and must be awakened." But there was a major problem. Anything God placed His attention on would become real. If He entered the dream to redeem His Son, the dream itself could become real to Him, trapping Him within it. This would risk eternal separation between Father and Son. If God acknowledged anything except perfect Oneness, then there would no longer *be* perfect Oneness. To solve this, God created a special agent, the Holy Spirit, a bridge between the two states of existence as the answer to the perceived separation. The Holy Spirit held the miraculous ability to view God's perfect Heaven while also seeing the Son's imperfect dream. The Holy Spirit recognized that Christ's Mind had plunged into a void, creating a black hole, attempting to disappear into nothingness. His fear was *that* immense. The Voice for God showed Christ His forgotten memory of Heaven, He remembered God's eternal Love, forgave Himself and His perfect Love for God exploded into His consciousness. He woke up in the Heaven He had never left.

Now Christ, once again learning from the Father, reflects, "I've gained much wisdom from my first question, "Whoa, why is this?"' I must now help the children I have made who are asleep." Thus, Jesus enters into the dream illusion. The Son envisions, "I will have Jesus be born of a virgin, and he will perform what my children will call miracles." Christ knows He has been healed by the Holy Spirit, so the same Spirit conceived Jesus in Mary's womb. Furthermore, Christ reasons, "I will ask the Holy Spirit to descend upon Jesus in the form of a dove after his baptism by John. Then, I will have him led into the desert immediately afterward, where he will live for forty days and nights without food or water." He understands that His children will mistakenly believe this is to be tempted by Satan, an entity that does not exist. Christ continues, "I will have Jesus trained in the wilderness to listen only to the Holy Spirit so that his ego will be completely eliminated. He will be the only one in time who will fully manipulate his dreaming. He will walk on water, calm the seas, feed the multitudes, teach magnificent spiritual truths, heal the paralyzed, restore sight to the blind, give hearing to the deaf, and, above all, raise the dead. This will prove to my children that death is an illusion, especially when he lives again after his crucifixion." Yet Christ knows His children will believe he died for their sins. "My Father knows nothing of my false universe and does not even know what sin is." He realizes, "I will have the same Holy Spirit who healed Me lead Jesus to fully understand that he is One with Me, just as I am One with Our Father. My creations will eventually comprehend the same truth."

This is the end of my little story and these are the implications. When the last mind is healed and our false universe dissolves, the Father and the Son will experience boundless joy in teaching Their beautiful children the perfection of their being. Forever. The Holy Spirit is in our minds healing us the exact same way by the exact same sequence. At first we are shown glimpses of our forgotten memory of Heaven. This has happened to me by reading several writings similar to "Intra Muros", I only mentioned Rebecca's dossier because it was by far the best. By believing these writings I began to remember God's eternal Love. Next, I started forgiving others, so in essence I was forgiving myself. When I have finally achieved perfection in forgiveness my perfect Love for God will also explode into my consciousness and I'll awaken in the Heaven I've never left. And so it is with you because this is God's Will.

CHAPTER 10

# Guilt

THERE SEEMS TO BE an endless cycle of guilt stories, appearing in different timelines within the script. Though they take on various forms, they always reinforce the same theme, you are guilty. Like steam rising from a pot of boiling water, these guilt-infused narratives continue to surface. We believe ourselves guilty for actions taken within the physical world, but every guilty thought is merely a reflection of the "tiny mad idea", the belief that we separated from God and destroyed Love. From this single illusion of separation, the ego's entire framework unfolds, an intricate system embedded with countless dream scripts, each designed to perpetuate guilt. These thoughts emerge in many forms: "I am guilty because I am not a good enough parent. I am guilty because I struggle to grasp The Course. I am guilty because my business failed. I am guilty because my partner left me, proving I am unworthy of Love." Whatever the specifics, they are unique to the individual's narrative, yet all stem from the same false belief in guilt.

When a guilty thought arises, it has nothing to do with form or the body, it is simply an attempt to reinforce the illusion of separation. The way to undo this illusion is to go directly to the core of the ego's program and disconnect it by affirming: "I am not guilty because I never separated from God. Nothing happened." How long will this process take? Will the cycle of guilt ever end? The ego insists upon punishment and condemnation, fueled by the belief in death and destruction of the body. However, Jesus states, "The world will end in an illusion, as it began. The purpose of forgiveness is complete, excluding no one, limitless in gentleness. It will cover it, hiding all evil, concealing all sin, and ending guilt forever. So ends the world that guilt had made, for now it has no purpose and is gone." The world itself was made by guilt, as revealed in ACIM Jesus highlights how forgiveness is quiet, it does nothing, merely looks, waits, and does not judge. It does not twist reality to fit preferred appearances but simply observes without resistance. Each time we engage in quiet observation, we unknowingly unravel guilt. Though we do not yet see how much remains, the path requires persistence. We must step away from the ceaseless exchange of guilt, pushing it onto others, only to have it erupt within our mind again. The ego entices us to hurl blame at our brothers, hoping to cleanse the false belief in sin within ourselves. We attempt to project guilt outward, convincing ourselves that it will relieve our own suffering.

Yet, as obstacles clear, we begin to recognize the mechanics of the ego, how its primary goal is to nourish the belief in guilt, keeping it alive like a ravenous wolf. Jesus describes this force with striking words, "The messengers of fear are harshly ordered to seek out guilt, and cherish every scrap of evil and of sin that they can find, losing none of them on pain of death. They lay them respectfully before their lord and master. Its messengers steal guiltily away in hungry search of guilt, for they are kept cold and starving and made very vicious by their master, who allows them to feast only upon what they return to him. No little shred of guilt escapes their hungry eyes. And in their savage search for sin, they pounce on any living thing they see and carry it screaming to their master, to be devoured." Jesus' potent words emphasize the brutal intensity of guilt. He intends for us to fully grasp its vicious grip. If you believe you are guilty, you will believe you deserve punishment. And the ego's punishment is death. To believe in guilt is to believe in death.

As you cultivate quiet time with the Holy Spirit, space begins to form between you and the thought of guilt. This space allows you to choose whether or not to engage with it. In the earlier stages, it may feel as though you must unwind and unravel every guilt-laden thought and emotion, like straightening out a tangled extension cord. The Holy Spirit, much like a vacuum, clears away these illusory guilt thoughts, leading you to the one core false belief: the idea that you separated from God. Once you recognize the "tiny mad idea" for what it is, that separation never occurred, you can disconnect from all guilt-based narratives embedded within the dream scripts of time. Affirm again, "I am not guilty because I never separated from God. Nothing happened. I am as God created me." Remember, as you undo guilt in your mind, you are undoing the world. Jesus offers these powerful words, "Prisoners bound with heavy chains for years, starved and emaciated, weak and exhausted, and with eyes so long cast down in darkness they remember not the light, do not leap up in joy the instant they are made free. It takes time for them to understand what freedom is. You groped but feebly in the dust and found your brother's hand, uncertain whether to let it go or to take hold of life so long forgotten. Strengthen your hold and raise your eyes unto your strong companion, in whom the meaning of your freedom lies. He seemed to be crucified beside you. And yet his Holiness remained untouched and perfect, and with him beside you, you shall this day enter with him to Paradise, and know the Peace of God." To undo guilt in the mind, you must observe it without judgment and forgive what never truly happened. A key component of this forgiveness process is taking responsibility for the mis-creation of the mind. Without this step, you are merely spinning your wheels. Let the Holy Spirit guide you in releasing all illusions, returning you to the truth of your eternal innocence. Now, let us reflect together and seek understanding of what this means for humanity.

CHAPTER 11

# What Does This All Mean?

AS I REFLECTED ON my thoughts, it became clear that we are destined to become Co-Creators with God. This realization emerged despite my ego's constant insistence that such an idea is sheer madness. Jesus explains in The Course that he is not meant to be worshiped, only deeply respected. The only difference between him and us is that what remains potential for us is already his Reality. He has God and nothing else. Over two thousand years ago, Jesus initiated the principle of the Atonement, At-One-Ment, the understanding we're not separate from Source. Imagine that you and I are strangers, enjoying a cold beer on a hot summer afternoon in a quiet little bar. We strike up a conversation, and after an hour, the alcohol has mildly set in. I say, "Our discussions have been enjoyable. I'd like you to know something about me." "What's that?" "I'm perfect." You suddenly remember an errand you need to run for your wife and realize you cannot miss dinner. While driving home, you think, "Wow, does that guy have issues, he needs professional therapy." However, suppose you happen to be God. The response would be, "Thank you, My Son. I know, because this is how I created you." If God created anything imperfect, He would no longer be perfect. Therefore, we are perfect. We may make mistakes in our dreams, but this does not negate our perfection in Heaven.

As mentioned several times, we will eventually evolve into Co-Creator God Consciousness Beings. This is a natural process, unfolding in its time. There is much we can learn by observing nature and her lessons. In nature, there is never a rush to accelerate a process, everything is always perfect in its moment. When the time is right, the rose will bloom. The Universal Christ Mind is constantly communicating with all creation. For the kingdoms without free will, this connection is known as innate intelligence, guidance that flows directly from the Universal Mind. It is what instructs the beaver to build a dam, the bird to weave a nest, a flock to fly in V formation, the spider to spin her web, and animals to hibernate through winter. The timing always arrives flawlessly. These life forms remain in Christ's presence at all times. This guidance is perfect, manifesting harmony, balance, order, and unity for the good of all. Nature comes together, embodying the synchronicity of Oneness as life unfolds. The mineral, plant, insect, animal, and angelic kingdoms do not possess free will; they are fully connected to the Christ Mind and maintain conscious awareness in every moment. Humanity, however, is also directly connected but has yet to learn how to remain consciously aware. Before arriving on earth, we were connected to the Son's Mind through innate intelligence. But upon entering this world, we were gifted with free will, the ability to manifest using a conscious mind and to discern through the five senses and reasoning. Once we understand that we are always connected to the Universal Mind, never separate from the Oneness of life, we will learn to trust our feelings and reconnect with the truth of our perfection.

Gary Renard's books are remarkable, and offer profound insights into forgiveness and spiritual awakening. In his writing, Gary explains, "Imagine you're watching TV and you forgive a news story you see. The Holy Spirit then spreads your forgiveness throughout the mind that projects the universe, and through the projection itself. This act cuts through unconscious guilt and its karmic projections like a laser beam, affecting all your past and future lives, every dimension of time, and every parallel universe that seems to exist." As forgiveness is practiced, the Holy Spirit collapses time, erasing lessons that would have otherwise needed to be learned. Although it may seem as though nothing is happening, something extraordinary *is* unfolding. By forgiving all that has occurred in the imagined past, untruth is unlearned, and the memory of being God's Child begins to return, healing the mind. As mentioned in the preface, the ego is like an onion, peeling away one layer still leaves an onion that looks and smells the same. But with persistent forgiveness, vast layers of the ego are stripped away, and eventually, the ego itself disappears. When the final layer is gone, the ego is undone, leaving nothing to interfere with the experience of Who You Are. There is no longer a reason to reincarnate within the dream. True forgiveness continues to guide the way out of the cycle of birth and death. Perhaps a close friend was planning to steal from you tomorrow, but this does not happen. The reason? You had already forgiven a close friend who had stolen in the past. A lesson learned does not need repeating. You might wonder what happens to someone like the serial killer Jeffrey Dahmer at the moment of death. According to what I have read, each soul is accompanied by two or three spiritual advisors who review their life experiences after transitioning from the body. They are shown both the good and the bad. At this point, they are asked, "Would you prefer to return to a body?" With a now properly functioning mind a mass murderer would respond, "I lived a terrible life and now understand the immense suffering I caused, especially to the loved ones of my victims. I need to return as a baby and endure torture and death to truly grasp the horror I inflicted." Reincarnation, experienced within our dream, serves as a mechanism for continued learning, allowing souls to correct past mistakes and ultimately attain perfection in forgiveness.

Each time a baby appears to be born into this world, it is merely reliving the moment when it seemed to leave its perfect environment in God, where all was Nirvana, where it was completely cared for and provided for, only to suddenly find itself thrust into a reality that feels like a living hell by comparison. Birth is often considered a miracle, yet babies do not enter the world smiling. They arrive crying and screaming. The mind that is reliving the seeming separation has fallen asleep and is dreaming an idle, insignificant dream, or a nightmare, because anything that appears apart from Heaven must symbolize its opposite. It must include opposing characteristics. There is no doubt that we believe we are experiencing reality here, but we must be shown the way out. Our "asleep at the wheel" mind does not realize it, but it is destined to wake up in the equivalent of a cosmic instant. The Voice for God and Heaven, the Holy Spirit, is always present, reminding us of the truth and calling us to return. This fail-safe memory of who we truly are can never be lost, making an awakening to the Reality of Heaven inevitable. We have the power to choose the memory and strength of God or something else instead. That is the choice the mind made immediately after the seeming separation. Out of shock, fear, and confusion, it made a series of unwise decisions that resulted in our appearance here. Yet we still do not realize that, given the remarkable power of the mind, certain choices could end the seeming separation at any time. This means we are capable of accomplishing it, with the beautiful help of the Holy Spirit. God could not have created this world, it would not be in His nature, for He is not cruel. If this were the real world, God would be cruel, for no loving Father could subject His children to such suffering as the price of salvation. Jesus told the parable of the Prodigal Son, a king's son took his vast inheritance and traveled to a far-off land, squandering his wealth on wine and pleasure. Eventually, he became destitute and realized, "My father's servants live far better than this. I will return and beg for forgiveness. Perhaps he will allow me to work in his vineyard." The king, upon learning of his son's return, declared, "Prepare a feast, for my son was lost but now is found." Recently, I considered the possibility that Christ was the first Prodigal Son. After His healing, He must have gained a new understanding, He knew what it *felt* like to be forgiven. Although God does not forgive, for He sees nothing *to* forgive, Christ experienced the feeling of restoration.

When I consider the world's endless temptations, peace is the only one that draws me now. Nothing else makes sense to me anymore. Peace brings the awareness of God's Love. I am the perfect, loving, and limitless extension of God. Only my thoughts and beliefs could convince me otherwise. All I need to do is remain in the peace and silence of this present moment. Everything else fades from my awareness, leaving only God's Love and Peace. These truths were always present, shining brightly in the background of my mind, no longer obscured by the meaningless thoughts and illusions of the ego. Do not let the clouds of delusion conceal the Light of your Being. Simply *be* the Light, for you *are* the Light you seek. The following chapters come directly from The Course and enforce the previous thoughts. Who is Christ? Who is the Holy Spirit? What is the Second Coming? What is the Final Judgment? What is creation? Who am I? What is Salvation? What is the Body? What is Jesus's purpose? What is the World? The Ancient Song.

# CHAPTER 12

# Who Is Christ?

"Christ is God's Son as He created Him. He is the Self we share, uniting us with one another, and with God as well. He is the Thought which still abides within the Mind that is His Source. Furthermore, He has not left His Holy home, nor lost the innocence in which He was created. He abides unchanged forever in the Mind of God. Christ is the link that keeps you one with God and guarantees that separation is no more than an *illusion* of despair, for hope will forever abide in Him. Your mind is part of His, and His of yours. He is the part in which God's Answer lies; where all decisions are already made, and dreams are over. He remains untouched by anything the body's eyes perceive. For though in Him His Father placed the means for your salvation, yet does He remain the Self, Who like His Father, knows no sin. Home of the Holy Spirit, and at home in God alone, does Christ remain at peace within the Heaven of your Holy mind. This is the only part of you that has Reality in Truth. The rest are dreams.

Yet will these dreams be given into Christ, to fade before His glory and reveal your Holy Self, the Christ, to you at last. The Holy Spirit reaches from the Christ in you to all your dreams and bids them come to Him, to be translated into Truth. He will exchange them for the final dream, which God appointed as the end of dreams. For when forgiveness rests upon the world and peace has come to every Son of God, what could there be to keep things separate, for what remains to see except Christ's face? And how will this Holy face be seen, when it is but the symbol that the time for learning now is over, and the goal of the Atonement has been reached at last? So, therefore, let us seek Christ's face and look at nothing else. As we behold His glory, will we know we have no need of learning or perception or of time, or anything except the Holy Self, the Christ Whom God created as His Son."

CHAPTER 13

# Who Is The Holy Spirit?

"The Holy Spirit mediates between illusions and the Truth. Since he must bridge the gap between Reality and dreams, perception leads to knowledge through the grace that God has given Him, to be His gift, to everyone who turns to Him for Truth. Across the bridge that He provides are dreams all carried to the Truth, to be dispelled before the light of knowledge. There are sights and sounds forever laid aside, and where they were perceived before, forgiveness has made possible perception's tranquil end. The goal of the Holy Spirit's teachings is just this end of dreams. For sights and sounds must be translated from the witness of fear to those of Love. And when this is entirely accomplished, learning has achieved the only goal it has in Truth. For learning as the Holy Spirit guides it to the outcome He perceives for it, becomes the means to go beyond itself, to be replaced by the eternal Truth.

If you but knew how much your Father yearns to have you recognize your sinlessness, you would not let His Voice appeal in vain, nor turn away from His replacement for the fearful images and dreams you made. The Holy Spirit understands the means you made by which you would attain what is forever unattainable. And if you offer them to Him, He will employ the means you made for exile to restore your mind to where it truly is at Home. From knowledge, where He has been placed by God, the Holy Spirit calls to you, to let forgiveness rest upon your dreams and be restored to sanity and peace of mind. Without forgiveness, will your dreams remain to terrify you. And the memory of all your Father's Love, will not return to signify the end of dreams has come. Accept your Father's gift. It is a call from Love to Love, that it be but Itself. The Holy Spirit is His gift by which the quietness of Heaven is restored to God's beLoved Son. Would you refuse to take the function of completing God, when all He wills is that you be complete?"

The Holy Spirit descended on Jesus in the form of a dove after he was baptized by John.

CHAPTER 14

# What Is The Second Coming?

"Christ's Second Coming, which is sure as God, is merely the correction of mistakes and the return of sanity. It is a part of the condition that restores the never lost and reestablishes what is forever and forever true. It is the invitation to God's Word to take the illusion's place; the willingness to let forgiveness rest upon all things without exception and without reserve. Furthermore, it is the all-inclusive nature of Christ's Second Coming that permits it to embrace the world and hold you safe within its gentle advent, which encompasses all living things with you. There is no end to the release the Second Coming brings, as God's Creation must be limitless. Forgiveness lights the Second Coming's way because it shines on everything as one. And thus is Oneness recognized at last.

The Second Coming ends the lessons that the Holy Spirit teaches, making way for the Last Judgment, in which learning ends in one last summary that will extend beyond itself and reaches up to God. The Second Coming is the time in which all minds are given to the hands of Christ, to be returned to Spirit in the name of true Creation and the Will of God. The Second Coming is the one event in time which time itself cannot affect. For everyone, whoever came to die, or yet will come, or who is present now, is equally released from what he made. In this equality is Christ restored as One Identity, in which the Sons of God acknowledge that they are One. And God the Father smiles upon his Son, His One Creation and His only joy. Pray that the Second Coming will be soon, but do not rest with that. It needs your eyes and ears and hands and feet. It requires your voice, and most of all, it requires your willingness. Let us rejoice that we can do God's Will and join together in His Holy light. Behold, the Son of God is One in us, and we can reach our Father's Love through Him."

CHAPTER 15

# What Is The Final Judgment?

"Christ's Second Coming gives the Son of God this gift: To hear the Voice of God proclaim that what is false is false, and what is true has never changed. And this judgment is where perception ends. At first, you see a world that has accepted this as true, projected from a now-corrected mind. And with this Holy sight, perception gives silent blessings and then disappears, its goal accomplished and its mission done. The Final Judgment on the world contains no condemnation. For it sees the world as forgiven, without sin, and wholly purposeless. Without a cause, and now without a function in Christ's sight, it merely slips away to nothingness. There it was born, and there it ends as well. And all the figures in the dream in which the world began go with it. Bodies now are useless, and all will therefore fade away because the Son of God is limitless. You who believed that God's Last Judgment would condemn the world to Hell along with you, accept this Holy Truth: God's Judgment is the gift of Correction He bestowed on all your errors, freeing you from them and all effects they ever seemed to have. To fear God's saving grace is but to fear complete release from suffering, return to peace, security, happiness, and union with your own Identity. God's Final Judgment is as merciful as every step in His appointed plan to bless His Son and call Him to return to the eternal peace He shares with Him. Be not afraid of Love. For it alone can heal all sorrow, wipe away all tears, and gently waken from his dream of pain the Son whom God acknowledges as His. Be not afraid of this. Salvation asks you to give it a welcome. And the world awaits your glad acceptance, which will set it free. This is God's Final Judgment: "You are still My Holy Son, forever innocent, forever loving, and forever Loved, as limitless as your Creator, and completely changeless and forever pure. Awaken and return to Me. I am your Father and you are My Son."

CHAPTER 16

# What Is Creation?

"Creation is the sum of all God's Thoughts, infinite in number, and everywhere without all limits. Only Love creates, and only like Itself. There was no time when all that It created was not there. Nor will there be a time when anything It created suffers any loss. Forever and forever are God's Thoughts exactly as they were and as they are, unchanged through time and after time is done. God's Thoughts are given all the power that their own Creator has. For He would add to Love by its extension. Thus, His Son shares in Creation, and must therefore share in the power to create. What God has willed to be forever One will still be One when time is over, and will not be changed over time, remaining as it was before the thought of time began. Creation is the opposite of all illusions, for Creation is the Truth. Creation is the Holy Son of God, for in Creations is His Will complete in every aspect, making every part container of the Whole. Its Oneness is forever guaranteed inviolate; forever held within His Holy Will, beyond all possibility of harm, separation, imperfection, and of any spot upon its sinlessness. We are Creation; we are the Sons of God. We seem to be discrete, and unaware of our eternal unity with Him. Yet back of all our doubts, past all our fears, there still is a certainty. For Love remains with all Its Thoughts, Its sureness being theirs. God's memory is in our Holy minds, which know their Oneness and their unity with their Creator. Let our function be only to let this memory return, only to let God's Will be done on earth, only to be restored to sanity, and to be but as God created us. Our Father calls to us, We hear His Voice, and we forgive Creation in the Name of its Creator, Holiness Itself, Holiness His Creation shares; Whose Holiness is still a part of us."

CHAPTER 17

# Who Am I?

"I Am God's Son, complete and healed and whole, shining in the reflection of His Love. In me is His Creation sanctified and guaranteed eternal Life. In me is Love perfected, fear impossible, and joy established without opposite. I am the Holy Home of God Himself. I am the Heaven where His Love resides. I Am His Holy Sinlessness Itself, for in my purity abides His Own. Our use for words is almost over now. Yet in the final days of this one year we gave to God together, you and I, we found a single purpose that we shared. And thus you're joined with me, so what I am is you as well. The Truth of what we are is not for words to speak of nor describe. Yet, we can realize our function here, and words can speak of this and teach it, too, if we exemplify the words in us. We are the bringers of salvation. We accept our part as saviors of the world, which through our joint forgiveness is redeemed. And this, our gift, is therefore given to us. We look on everyone as brothers, and perceive all things as kindly and as good. We do not seek a function that is past the gate of Heaven. knowledge will return when we have done our part. We are concerned only with giving welcome to the Truth. Ours are the eyes through which Christ's vision sees a world redeemed from every thought of sin. Ours are the ears that hear the Voice for God proclaim the world as sinless. Not only that, but ours are the minds that join together as we bless the world. And from the Oneness that we have attained, we call to all our brothers, asking them to share our peace and consummate our joy. We are the Holy Messengers of God who speak for Him, and carrying His Word to everyone whom He has sent to us, we learn that it is written on our Hearts. And thus our minds are changed about the aim for which we came, and which we seek to serve. We bring glad tidings to the Son of God, who thought he suffered. And as he sees the gate of Heaven stand open before him, he will enter in and disappear into the Heart of God." Jesus

Awakening is not accomplished through the death of the body. Our Soul is eternal and cannot die. Therefore, if our Soul is not awakened at the point in time when we drop the physical body, it will simply create another body in which to continue its journey to awakening. Yet one thing is certain, as promised by God. We will awaken to the Truth that we are exactly as God created us. What we are experiencing now is being awake within the dream. Soon, we will awaken from the dream. Bob

# CHAPTER 18

# What Is Salvation?

"Salvation is a promise made by God that you would find your way to Him at last. It cannot but be kept. It guarantees that time will have an end and all the thoughts that have been born in time will end as well. God's word is given to every mind which thinks that it has separate thoughts, and will replace these thoughts of conflict with the Thought of peace. The Thought of peace was given to God's Son the instant that his mind had thought of war. There was no need for such a Thought before, for peace was given without opposite, and merely was. But when the mind is split, there is a need for healing. So the Thought that has the power to heal the split became a part of every fragment of the mind that was still One, but failed to recognize its Oneness. now it did not know itself and thought its own identity was lost. Salvation is undoing in the sense that it does nothing, failing to support the world of greed and malice. Thus, it lets illusions go by not supporting them, it merely lets them quietly go down to dust. And what they hid is now revealed; an altar to the Holy Name of God whereon His Word is written, with the gifts of your forgiveness laid before it, and the memory of God not far behind. Let us come daily to this Holy place, and spend a while together. Here we share our final dream. It is a dream in which there is no sorrow, for it holds a hint of all the glory given us by God. The grass is pushing through the soil, the trees are budding now, and birds have come to live within their branches. Earth is being born again from a new perspective. Night is gone, and we have come together in the light. From here we give salvation to the world, for here salvation was received. The song of our rejoicing is our call to all the world that freedom is returned, that time is almost over, and God's Son has but an instant more to wait until his Father is remembered. Dreams are done, Eternity has shone away the world, and only Heaven exists." Salvation is transcendence.

# CHAPTER 19

# What Is The Body?

"The body is a fence the Son of God imagines he has built to separate parts of his Self from other parts. It is within this fence he lives, to die as it decays and crumbles. For within this fence he thinks that he is safe from Love. Identifying with his safety, he regards himself as what his safety is. How else could he be certain he remains within the body, keeping Love outside? The body will not stay. Yet, this he sees as double safety. For the Son of God's impermanence is "proof" his fences work and do the task his mind assigns to them. For if his Oneness still remained untouched, who could attack and who could be attacked? Who could be Victor? Who could be his prey? Who could be the victim? Who is the murderer? And if he did not die, what proof is there that God's eternal Son could be destroyed?

    The body is a dream. Like other dreams, it sometimes seems to picture happiness. But can quite suddenly revert to fear, where every dream is born. For only Love creates in Truth, and Truth can never fear. Made to be fearful, must the body serve the purpose given it. But we can change the purpose that the body will obey by changing what we think that it is for. The body is the means by which God's Son returns to sanity. Though it was made to fence him into Hell without escape, yet has the goal of Heaven been exchanged for the pursuit of Hell. The Son of God extends his hand to reach his brother and to help him walk along the road with him. Now the body is Holy. Now it serves to heal the mind that it was made to kill. You will identify with what you think will make you safe. Whatever it may be, you will believe that it is one with you. Your safety lies in Truth and not in lies. Love is your safety. Fear does not exist. Identify with Love and you are safe. Identify with Love and you are Home. Identify with Love and find yourself."

# CHAPTER 20

# What Is Jesus' Purpose?

"This Jesus, once again, is on an entirely different level than the body called Jesus which is portrayed in the gospels. As such, the name of Jesus is but a symbol, but One that stands for the Love that is not of this world. In "A Course In Miracles", Jesus speaks about himself: I am responsible for the process of Atonement, which I undertook to begin, two thousand years ago in the region of Palestine. The figure we call Jesus manifested this Atonement principle, by virtue of introducing to people the idea that identity is not about a body, but about Spirit. Jesus clarifies it that in essence, he does not differ from us, and that he should be regarded as an elder brother. An elder brother is entitled to respect for his greater experience and obedience for his greater wisdom."

CHAPTER 21

# What Is The World?

"The world is a hypnotic enslavement for God's Son, keeping him bound by his own thinking and thoughts. It is a dry and dusty place where starved and thirsty creatures come to die. The purpose of the world as stated in "A Course In Miracles" is for it to be used to correct our unbelief. Jesus asks that we use the world to heal the separation. We repurpose the world and use it to learn forgiveness. So now the world becomes your multidimensional classroom to learn that you never left God and that the separation was healed. Through the Holy Spirit, the world is used as a teaching device for bringing you Home. The world is an illusory realm where God's Son, that's you, Awakens to his eternal Innocence. The world is not left by death but by Truth, and Truth can be known by all those for whom the Kingdom was created, and for whom it waits."

# CHAPTER 22

# The Ancient Song

"Beyond the body, beyond the sun and stars, past everything you see and yet somehow familiar, is an arc of golden light that stretches as you look into a great and shining circle. And all the circle fills with light before your eyes. The edges of the circle disappear, and what is in it is no longer contained at all. The light expands and covers everything, extending to infinity, forever shining and with no break or limit anywhere. Within it, everything is joined in perfect continuity. Nor is it possible to imagine that anything could be outside, for there is nowhere that this light is not. This is the vision of the Son of God, whom you know well. Here is the sight of Him who knows his Father. Here is the memory of what you are, a part of this, with all of it within and joined to all as surely as all is joined to you. Accept the vision that can show you this, and not the body. You know the ancient song and know it well. Nothing will ever be as dear to you as is this ancient hymn of Love the Son of God sings to his Father still."

CHAPTER 23

# Mutant Message Down Under

Marlo Morgan's "Mutant Message Down Under" presents a fascinating account of her experiences with the Aboriginal people of Australia. She was a healthcare professional who had done extensive charitable work for the Aborigines. After years of service, she was granted an honor never before offered, an invitation to an awards ceremony deep in the Australian desert. Upon arrival, she was asked to relinquish all her possessions. Her clothes, wallet, and credit cards were burned, and she was given traditional attire. The Chief extended an extraordinary invitation—to live with them for three moons, or three months, in the desert. She accepted, but after the first day of walking, doubts crept in. Her feet were bloodied and blistered from walking barefoot. The women applied natural salves, which healed her wounds more effectively than any pharmaceutical treatment. By the next day, she was walking pain-free, her feet quickly becoming calloused. What she witnessed was astounding. The tribe communicated through telepathy. One day, the Chief abruptly stopped the group, having received a telepathic message. A hunter had fallen ill after killing a kangaroo and requested permission to cut off the tail to lighten the load. Days later, he arrived at camp with the tailless kangaroo, severely sick. Two weeks later, a man fell from a thirty-foot cliff, shattering his femur. The bone had broken through the skin, snapped in two. Marlo observed the tribe's healer at work. After applying the same salve, she placed her hands around the injury. Astonishingly, an energy of light radiated from her hands, mending the bone and sealing the wound. The next day, the man was walking as if nothing had happened. Marlo witnessed many other extraordinary occurrences, each reinforcing the tribe's deep Spiritual connection. The Aborigines own no property or homes, yet they are remarkably healthy and live long lives. Their society experiences no wars, crime, prisons, hospitals, governments, or drug problems. They refer to outsiders as "mutants", people who live sheltered lives with little or no interest in God.One of the most valuable lessons she learned was how they pray. Each morning, they petition, "Great Spirit, for my highest good and the highest good of all, please help us find sustenance to survive." They live in the heart of a vast, desolate desert.

Fifteen years ago, I faced bankruptcy and lost two properties. Forced to rent, I was informed after two years that I had to move because the rental was being sold. To make matters worse, my unemployment had just ended. My credit rating was shattered, and no rental complex would approve me. Desperate, I recalled "Mutant Message Down Under" and decided to try the prayer. I prayed, "Holy Spirit, for my highest good and the highest good of all, please find me a job and a place to live." That very day, I accepted employment and was approved for an apartment. Prayer must come from the heart. The Holy Spirit knows what is truly needed. If one prays for a new car, it is unlikely anything will happen. Recently, I began a nightly prayer, especially when my mind is restless. I pray, "Holy Spirit, for my highest good and the highest good of all, please grant perfection in listening to the Sacred Silence between my thoughts."Try this. You may not immediately experience what I do, but you will find yourself asking fewer questions and developing a growing awareness of God's infinite Love and Peace. A peaceful mind is no small gift. Remember, God is changeless and Loves you the same today as He did the moment you were born. Our growing awareness is a great blessing, a miracle. As we learn to Love ourselves, knowing we were created by Love, we begin to extend unconditional Love to others. Always give to those in need, expecting nothing in return. A peaceful mind should also be extended by never allowing oneself to become upset. When someone strikes, physically or verbally, they expect retaliation. When you do not respond in kind, you disrupt their expectations. Perhaps, if they find themselves in a similar situation later, they will remember your response and act differently. This is what Jesus meant when he spoke of "Turning the other cheek".

CHAPTER 24

# Ayahuasca

I PROPOSED TO JAMIE on a July 4th weekend after flying to North Carolina. Unfortunately, our relationship fell apart when Jamie realized something I had yet to understand. I was still deeply in Love with Mary Jo. Jamie's girlfriend was dating a pilot who always traveled to North Carolina over the Fourth for traditional reunions with old friends. We arrived at a beautiful oceanfront condominium and met James, one of the most fascinating individuals I had ever encountered. He owned an internet company with over eighty employees. When I asked what he marketed, he explained that they had initially worked with Disney but had no success. Eventually, they shifted to adult content, and the company became highly profitable. James had been raised in a strict Christian environment and was very close to his sister. At her wedding, whispers followed him, "There's the porn king." He told us he watches a little now and then but sees it as his livelihood. He resented how some Christians judged him. I completely agreed.

The three of us talked all night, and James shared one of the most incredible stories I had ever heard. He and a close friend had each paid five thousand dollars to fly to Peru and spend a week with a Shaman in the jungle. Their purpose was to take Ayahuasca, the most powerful hallucinogen on the planet. They were instructed to fast for three days before taking the drug. Exactly as the Shaman had predicted, after half an hour, they vomited. Then, the hallucinations began. James was confronted with his ego, its vast, chaotic insane intelligence laid bare before him. The vision was so overwhelming that he abandoned any attempt to reason with it and simply observed. This mirrored "A Course in Miracles", which teaches that engaging with the ego only reinforces its false Reality.

Next came the revelation. James saw how everything is interconnected. His vision expanded beyond comprehension, multi-universes, galaxies, stars, countless worlds, molecules, atoms, all life, all existence,created and sustained by an all-encompassing, intelligent, eternal, Loving Force. And there was nowhere this Force was not. James fell silent for a moment before saying, "Death is an illusion. We live forever." Everything he described could have come straight from "A Course in Miracles", yet he had never heard of the manuscript. The experience profoundly affected his friend, who remained in Peru for several months. A professional painter, his art was later exhibited at the United Nations. James shared that the Shamans had been instructed to reveal their wisdom to humanity, though he did not say by whom. I find it miraculous that two indigenous cultures, the Aborigines and the Shamans, are now sharing ancient wisdom with the world.

CHAPTER 25

# Jonathan Livingston Seagull

JONATHAN LIVINGSTON SEAGULL, WRITTEN by Richard Bach in 1970, is a deeply Spiritual and philosophical story about a seagull named Jonathan who seeks to perfect his flying skills rather than conform to the ordinary life of his flock. The book became a New York Times bestseller and has been widely regarded as an allegory for self-discovery, transcendence, and the pursuit of higher knowledge. As a young gull, Jonathan lived like all the others, fighting for scraps of fish thrown from boats. But as he grew older, he realized there had to be more to life than mere survival. He began practicing flight, refining his techniques, and pushing the limits of speed and aerodynamics. His dedication made him an outcast among his flock, but he remained undeterred. He mastered wing trim, spin dives, tail dives, and advanced aerial maneuvers. His speed allowed him to dive deep for the best fish and soar high for insects. Jonathan lived a long life, but one day, while flying, a baby gull crossed his path. He swerved and collided with a cliff at high speed. At that moment, he transitioned to another existence, where the Great Gull stood beside him and said, "Well, Jonathan, your method of leaving time was a little abrupt. Let's continue your training." Jonathan soon reached a state where he could think of a place and instantly be there.

This story carries profound meaning. Jonathan's relentless pursuit of perfection in flight allowed him to live better than the other gulls. His journey mirrors the Spiritual path of those who seek higher understanding beyond societal norms. As a Christian, I see parallels between Jonathan's journey and the life of Jesus. Jesus lived a perfect life, embodying kindness, generosity, Truthfulness, forgiveness, and Love. His only adversaries were the religious hierarchy. If humanity embraced his teachings, particularly "Do unto others as you would have others do unto you", the world would transform. Wars, prisons, poverty, crime, and homelessness would cease to exist. Locks and passwords would become unnecessary. A simple principle, yet one that holds the power to change everything. Think about it, it's true.

## CHAPTER 26

# The Field

THE FIELD OPERATES AS a unified whole, instantly correlating distant events and holding memory of all that has transpired. It exists beyond time and space, creating and expanding within itself in an evolutionary direction. It is conscious. Without death, there can be no present moment, for each passing instant must dissolve to make way for the next. Without change, there can be no new Love, for each emotion must fade to allow another to emerge. Beyond fear and doubt, our deepest prayer should not be for life, which is already abundant. Instead, it should be a prayer to lead the cosmic dance, to move in harmony with the unfolding presence of creation. The Field is God.

CHAPTER 27

# Buddha

BUDDHA WAS PASSING THROUGH a village where the people began shouting insults, using every harsh word they could muster. Yet, Buddha simply stood there, listening silently and attentively. Then, he spoke. "Thank you for coming to me, but I am rushing, I must reach the next village, where people are waiting for me. I cannot devote more time to you today, but tomorrow, when I return, I will have more time. You can gather again, and if there is anything left unsaid, you may say it then. For now, please excuse me." The villagers were stunned. They had expected anger, humiliation, or at least retaliation. Yet this man remained utterly unaffected, undistracted. One among them asked, "Have you not heard us? We have been abusing you, and you have not even responded." Buddha smiled and said, "If you seek an answer, then you have come too late. You should have come ten years ago, then I would have answered. But I have long since stopped being manipulated by others. I am no longer a slave to reaction. I am my own master. I act according to my own nature, not in response to anyone else's. You cannot force me to do anything. It is perfectly fine that you wanted to insult me, you have done your task well. But as for me, I do not accept your insults. And unless I accept them, they are meaningless." When someone insults you, you must first accept their words, become a receiver, before you can react. But if you refuse to receive the insult, if you remain detached, what power does it have? Buddha explained, "If someone throws a burning torch into the river, they will watch it blaze until it touches the water. The moment it falls into the river, all fire is extinguished. The river cools it. I have become like the river, you throw insults at me, and they burn as they leave your lips. But the moment they reach me, their fire is lost. They no longer hurt. You throw thorns at me, yet falling into my silence, they become flowers. I act only from my own nature." Ever listened impartially to two people locked in an argument? Neither truly hears the other because each is consumed with forming a response. When the dispute finally ends, does either feel victorious? Is there ever a true winner? When listening to two egos justifying themselves, insanity is revealed. Never argue.

## CHAPTER 28

# Joyless Place

How else can you find joy in a joyless place except by realizing that you are not there? You cannot be anywhere God did not put you, and God created you as part of Him. That is both where you are and what you are. It is completely unalterable. It is total inclusion. You cannot change it now or ever. It is forever true. It is not a belief but a Fact. Anything that God created is as True as He is. The truth lies only in its perfect inclusion in Him.

CHAPTER 29

# Osho

OSHO'S TEACHINGS ON SANYAS emphasize the process of shedding the layers of illusion, the smoke, that obscure the inner flame of Love. He describes how memories, thoughts, desires, and imagination form a dense barrier around this light, preventing clarity and true understanding. The only way to reach the flame is to let go of these attachments, allowing the smoke to disperse naturally. Sanyas, as Osho explains, is about becoming silent and desireless, as if there is nothing to achieve and nowhere to go. In this state of relaxation, the mind ceases to feed the illusions, and they dissolve on their own. As the smoke clears, brightness, intelligence, and meaning emerge, filling life with significance. Love, when fully realized, radiates outward, touching others in a tangible way. It becomes a blessing not only to oneself but to the world. A true individual enriches existence, contributing to the greater whole. Without contribution, bliss remains elusive. Through giving, one participates in the work of the Creator, becoming a Co-Creator. This aligns with The Course, where the Holy Spirit is described as the force that undoes the ego, the false self that clings to illusions. Osho's concept of Sanyas mirrors this process, guiding one toward the recognition of their true nature beyond the limitations of the mind.

CHAPTER 30

# Awakening

I POSTED THIS PRAYER from the Course on Christmas. "Watch with me, angels, watch with me today. Let all God's Holy Thoughts surround me, and be still with me while Heaven's Son is born. Let earthly sounds be quiet, and the sights to which I am accustomed disappear. Let Christ be welcomed where He is at home. And let Him hear the sounds He understands, and sights that show His Father's Love. Let Him no longer be a stranger here, for He is born again in me today. Your Son is welcome, Father. He has come to save me from the evil self I made. He is the Self that You have given me. He is, but what I really am in truth. He is the Son You Love above all things. He is my Self as You created me. It is not Christ that can be crucified. Safe in Your Arms, let me receive Your Son. Amen." I've read in "Disappearance Of The Universe" that our job is to save God's Son. What higher calling could we possibly have? So *perhaps* the all powerful awakened Christ put a sleeping snippet of Himself in all of us. As we take care of and nurture the Christ Child within us, eventually He'll wake up, go Home and take us with Him. Thus, we have saved God's Son and we wake up as well.

CHAPTER 31

## Live In The Eternal Now

AT THIS MOMENT, YOU exist in the living Now. Only in the eternal present can you truly experience the reality of Love. Only here, in this moment, can your entire being manifest across all levels and dimensions. In the living Now, where the fiery act of creation brings forth life, you can fully recognize yourself as perfect Love, forever. You are the Heart of God, the very energies of creation. You and your Twin Flame Self are streams of Divine Masculine and Divine Feminine life. Only in perfect unity, right Now, can you experience the truth, that you are Love in its purest form, forever aware of yourself in relationship with all existence. beloved one, though I speak to you, my words are meant for all. You have embarked upon a new request for awareness, and I respond. This request arrives at the perfect time, unfolding the next step. This step was revealed to you recently through words carrying the keys to everything, words that lifted your heart and brought remembrance to life. You are as I created you, and this truth can never be altered.

Beloved Heart of All Love, I ask you now to surrender. Release all contradictions and embrace the one Real truth. If life on Earth is an illusion, a dream, then the Being you truly are has remained untouched by it. The experience of living on Earth has not changed who you are. Right now, in this moment, you are whole, vast, magnificent, the very expression of My own Twin Flame life. You are alive within My Heart. Within your heart, as well as Mine, exists the great creation of Love, now perfectly reflected everywhere. Each of you, precious living Twin Flame cells, "atoms" within My own great Heart, can release the dream of limited human life only by returning to the ever-living Now. The source of life and Love, the birthplace of creation, is not a beginning but the revelation of what has always existed. All that appears has simply been illuminated so that I may know Myself. Now, it is time for you to know yourselves as well, not the small human identity but the true purpose of your existence, beloved one, I reveal to you the answer to your questions: (a) The Reconnecting Process, as it relates to releasing your identity as a limited human being. (b) The way to manifest this understanding within yourself, including the revelation that energies within you have yet to fully accept the shift. This is evident because, if all your energies were fully aligned, the world around you would reflect perfect harmony. Some energies within you remain hidden, often referred to as subconscious, where the ego-mind conceals its workings and the beliefs of the heart. Yet, each time you ask, you turn on the light. If you are serious and attentive, the answers will emerge. For I am ever alive within you. You are My beating Heart. The pulse of life, the truth of your Being, always illuminates all that is brought into the River of Life and Light.

You have repeatedly asked to know the truth and to live it. You have agreed to bring forth the path, and I give My gratitude. Thus, I bring you the dream because it is a language you understand, a way to reveal subconscious beliefs. Now, you have awareness. You have reached the moment of recognition, the point where all that was hidden must be revealed so that you can choose. This choice defines your identity and your orientation to life. Will you remain entangled in duality, or will you dedicate yourself entirely to choosing only light, only life, only Love? The only way to return to your true identity as My Living Heart is to bring yourself fully into presence, to return to the Living Now Moment. Once you do, beloved one, all of you, then and only then can you experience and accept the truth of who you are. Once you have felt the reality of Twin Flame Love and lived the glorious explosion of life, only then can you claim it as your own, here and now.

The Reconnection Process begins with recognizing the false identity of a limited human existence, and transformation only comes through the Real. It is shifted in your Heart by experiencing truth at the center point in the Now. When this happens, your true identity must replace all illusions of separation, allowing you to live fully on Earth as well. In the living River of the Now moment of creation, the entire vertical arm of the cross is illuminated. The felt experience of being exactly as I created you dissolves the belief in humanness throughout your entire Being, including all hidden aspects, even the subconscious. Once this truth is felt, the shift is made. You have "gone vertical", as you say. You have moved the background into the foreground, using the language of the Real feelings. Most especially, the feeling of ecstatic joy and the unwavering assurance that I am ever and always with you, and that in Our Love, all life is embraced. This establishes your connection with the infinite flow of giving Love, the essential energy of your Real Twin Flame existence, ever-present in the ongoing Now. The key lies in the Now experience. Only by making yourself fully present can this shift take place. And this shift includes being the living Christ on Earth, not at some distant point in the future, after past struggles are resolved, but Now, in total surrender to Me, with every aspect of your human life. What you, and many others, have done is place everything away from you, setting healing in the future, postponing the shift into a Christ Being. Even though you have realized many things, you have not truly grasped this. Until now. Now you are ready. Your life moves forward like a rocket. You are already beyond the atmosphere.

I ask all of you to trust this. We are assembling everything, and it will happen all at once, your realizations, your readiness, the necessary people, and the resources. Surrender it all to Me. Move forward in every way "right now". Do not set any of it aside for the future, based on the constraints of the little mind. Everything is Now. including your full shift into the awakened Twin Flame Hearts you truly are. For all of you, I ask that you live the truth of the River of Life. There is only One, and from it flows your nourishment, your consciousness, your identity as Love Itself. The keys to moving forward as the living Heart of God are already in your grasp, so that I may Love as you, speak as you, and bring forth transformation. Transformation may appear as healing, but it is far more than physical restoration, it is all-encompassing, not limited to a single illness or injury. Your shift in identity is already underway. But, as always, you must choose. You must be conscious. You must be Love. The past and future are transformed by the Now. Everything you experience and accept at the center point extends into the hologram of your entire life, because you are One creative Twin Flame life. This is why transformation within a Twin Flame relationship instantly affects the other. There is truly only One of you. Only One of Us. To transform old Heart beliefs, consciously enter the Now, for only in the Now can the return to your true Self take place. Your identity through Me means feeling the joy of unlimited "Christedness". It means experiencing the center of your Twin Flame Heart, flowing in and out of one another in shared ecstasy. It means feeling the truth of your vast, limitless spirit and the perfect joy of your clear, open Heart. And it means knowing that this makes you available "right now" to act as Jesus did, and more. Bathe in the living River of Life, beyond all interpretations of the little mind. Simply stand in the truth of your Heart, and those you are meant to serve will be drawn to you like magnets, or like moths to a flame.

I have spoken to you before of acting as if it were already done, that you already *are* the Master. When you pray, pray in gratitude, knowing the miracles and accomplishments are already fulfilled. This is "going vertical", coming to the center to live and serve, offering shelter through the power of your Love. But know this: I need you to be at the center.

CHAPTER 32

# Time Is Collapsing

As the incoming light increases, you align with the truth of Love, becoming a column of living light. Anyone who enters this sacred presence will return to their true self. All infirmities will heal, hearts will open like roses, and the ego-mind will dissolve as if it never existed. This is what happened with Jesus, and now you are here to learn the same, to reveal the truth through the acceptance of the glorious Now moment and, most importantly, the acceptance of who you truly are. So, dear ones, your journey is to hold this, to stand firm at the center so that I Am in the world, expressed through you. Since you undertake this path for all humanity, there may be times when you shift back and forth between the Divine and the human, between the Real and life on Earth. I ask you to commit, to be unwavering in your dedication to holding the center by aligning with the vertical arm of truth. Be the Twin Flame opening through which Love flows into this world. If you find yourself caught once more in the identities of ego, return to the joy of the Now moment. Let it be real to you. Consciously shift, then center. Always do this from the Real. Trust the power of Love and recognize who you are, at the center, within the River. Practice this in meditation, before sleep, and upon waking, as these are moments when the little mind holds less influence. This is more than simply "acting as if", which often remains a mental exercise. This is about fully feeling exalted holy life. Your mind can serve as an arrow pointing toward the treasure, and your will can guide you to the center, but ultimately, you must surrender it. Imagination can assist, but it is through deep feelings that you reclaim your truth.

When you open the vertical arm fully and stand within its flow, all of life becomes available to you in that moment. Rather than rejecting life, the body, or existence in this world by retreating solely into consciousness, you will embrace *all* life, paving the way for the reclamation of humankind. The River of Life, the vertical arm, brings wholeness into the present, and My presence carries the message to all. Accept the One, the vertical, the identity as God, and everything is then drawn to the radiant force of your open and giving Heart. In the presence of one who has made this shift, hearts are cleared of the programs of consensual reality. The magnetic Twin Flame presence makes this possible. How? Just as a magnet held to a computer disc erases everything recorded there, so too does the presence of truth erase the illusion of a limited human identity. If any Twin Flame pair fully lives in the Now, then the column of light they hold instantly dissolves the false programs of reality. Gone. If the ego-mind attempts to reinstall them, the magnet restores truth again and again, effortlessly, simply through presence. "I Am Perfect Love, and I Am Perfect Life." Use these words as a launching pad into the living Now. Return to the center, beloved ones, and experience who you are as I created you. For you, our closeness will always reveal this truth. It will bring you the experience of who you truly are. The greatest call I ask of you is to return your projections from the future and your memories from the past, to bring everything back into the Now. Step into this eternal moment. Accept the Mantle of Christ.

CHAPTER 33

# The Gospel According To Thomas

The "Gospel According to Thomas" is an apocryphal, non-canonical text discovered in Nag Hammadi, Egypt, in December 1945, among a collection known as the Nag Hammadi Library. Written in the second century, it consists of 114 sayings attributed to the resurrected Jesus. Unlike the canonical gospels, it does not present a narrative but instead delivers teachings in concise, stand-alone statements. One passage conveys the nature of spiritual awakening, "Many stand at the threshold of their I Am awareness, yet do not know how to enter. Only the Solitary Ones pass into this bliss, for they unite soul, breath, and body into a singular purpose. Through surrendering the ego, they return to Oneness and reunite with the Living One. These will enter the Bridal Chamber, the Divine Temple, and in Heaven, they will awaken to new spiritual awareness. Their newly formed spiritual body will embody divine peace and rise into the Jerusalem consciousness of their individuality. This signifies the union of light consciousness with the earthly temple, the Bridegroom, the Christ Mind, taking residence with the Bride. Divine breath within the earthly form gives rise to the Child, and as one is born from Above, they become the Son of Man, comprehending this truth." The text warns against being one who lingers at the gate of Heaven, calling out but never stepping inside, "Do not be one known for much speaking, standing at Heaven's door, shouting, 'Let me in.' There is room only for the One. When will you cease believing in separation from Divine Being, as though you and It are apart? Listen, Children of God: Divine Consciousness is your consciousness, Divine Breath is your breath, and the Divine Heart beats within your heart. The life of our Divinity is One, expressed in infinite variety. There is no one besides God, anywhere." These words reflect a deep spiritual truth, emphasizing unity with God and the necessity of surrendering the ego to realize one's Divine Nature.

CHAPTER 34

# My Love, You Are So beloved

PLEASE NOTICE THE MESSAGES and signs being sent to you at this sacred and transformative time. You are receiving clear guidance from the Universe. All is not as it seems, higher processes are unfolding within and around you. My Love, you are deeply Loved. Even if everything feels chaotic, broken, or beyond repair, even if you feel alone, know that you are surrounded by Divine Love. Better days are coming. Not just better, but extraordinary, awe-inspiring, magical, soul-stirring, heart-expanding, spirit-ascending days. This is beyond the limits of your mind's understanding. It transcends your past experiences. The script of your life is being rewritten. The days of mediocrity, of feeling disconnected from your Heart, are fading. You are undergoing a profound and radical rebirth, being redefined, reconfigured, and renewed. Your Soul's Light is pouring into your energy centers like an unstoppable wave of transformation. You are being aligned with the path of Light. Your journey on Earth is about to shift dramatically, taking a course you never imagined. Even if everything feels wrong, in Divine truth, your life has never been more right. You are merging with your Soul, allowing it to guide you toward a life beyond your previous expectations. You are Loved beyond measure. Can you embrace Love this immense? It surpasses all human understanding. It is a Love that can only be expressed through the language of God, beyond the mortal mind. I Love you, I Love you, I Love you. Yes, you. You are worthy of everything. And it is arriving.     Sophie Bashford

CHAPTER 35

# Angels

IN ADDITION TO THE Trinity of the Father, Son, and Holy Spirit, there is another group of inhabitants in Heaven, the angels. "A Course in Miracles" mentions them sparingly, often as a secondary reference. This may seem contradictory, as the Course states that God created nothing besides the Son and that the universe consists solely of the Son of God. Yet, angels are acknowledged as existing. One of the few insights given about angels states, "You were created above the angels because your role involves creation as well as protection. You who are in the image of the Father need to bow only to Him, before whom I kneel with you." This suggests that the Son, humanity, is of a higher order than angels, as we are both Creators and protectors, whereas angels primarily serve as protectors.

After the fall into illusion, angels attempted to recover the separated ones but were unsuccessful. The Atonement began long before the crucifixion. Many souls offered their efforts to aid the separated ones, but they could not withstand the strength of the attack and had to be brought back. Angels also came, but their protection was insufficient, as the separated ones were not interested in peace. The only way to reconcile this contradiction is to view angels as part of the Sonship, fulfilling a distinct role. Ancient Wisdom teachings suggest that angels eventually become Sons of God. Other passages from the Course shed light on their purpose, "Your newborn purpose is nursed by angels, cherished by the Holy Spirit, and protected by God Himself. Around you, angels hover lovingly, keeping away all darkened thoughts of sin and preserving the Light where it has entered in. God's Name cannot be heard without response, nor spoken without an echo in the mind that calls you to remember. Say His Name, and you invite the angels to surround the ground on which you stand

and sing to you as they spread their wings. They keep you safe and shelter you from every worldly thought that would intrude upon your Holiness. You do not walk alone. God's angels hover near and all about. His Love surrounds you. He will never leave you comfortless, nor fail to send His angels down to answer you in His Own Name." These passages affirm the presence and role of angels in guiding, protecting, and assisting the Sonship on its journey back to God.

# CHAPTER 36

# The Egg

*The Egg by Andy Weir*

"You were on your way home when you died. It was a car accident. Nothing particularly remarkable, but fatal nonetheless. You left behind a wife and two children. It was a painless death. The EMTs tried their best to save you, but to no avail. Your body was so utterly shattered you were better off, trust Me. And that's when you met Me."

"What... what happened?" You asked. "Where am I?"

"You died," I said, matter-of-factly. No point in mincing words.

"There was a... a truck and it was skidding..."

"Yup," I said.

"I... I died?"

"Yup. But don't feel bad about it. Everyone dies," I said.

You looked around. There was nothingness. Just you and Me. "What is this place?" You asked. "Is this the afterlife?"

"More or less," I said.

"Are you God?" You asked.

"Yup," I replied. "I'm God."

"My kids... my wife," you said.

"What about them?"

"Will they be all right?"

"That's what I like to see," I said. "You just died, and your main concern is for your family. That's good stuff right there."

You looked at Me with fascination. To you, I didn't look like God. I just looked like some man. Or possibly a woman. Some vague authority figure, maybe. More of a grammar school teacher than the Almighty.

"Don't worry," I said. "They'll be fine. Your kids will remember you as perfect in every way. They didn't have time to grow contempt for you. Your wife will cry on the outside, but will be secretly relieved. To be fair, your marriage was falling apart. If it's any consolation, she'll feel very guilty for feeling relieved."

"Oh," you said. "So what happens Now? Do I go to Heaven or hell or something?"

"Neither," I said. "You'll be reincarnated."

"Ah," you said. "So the Hindus were right,"

"All religions are right in their own way," I said. "Walk with me."

You followed along as we strode through the void. "Where are we going?"

"Nowhere in particular," I said. "It's just nice to walk while we talk."

"So what's the point, then?" You asked. "When I get reborn, I'll just be a blank slate, right? A baby. So all my experiences and everything I did in this life won't matter."

"Not so!" I said. "You have within you all the knowledge and experiences of all your past lives. You just don't remember them right now."

I stopped walking and took you by the shoulders. "Your soul is more magnificent, beautiful, and gigantic than you can possibly imagine. A human mind can only contain a tiny fraction of what you *are*. It's like sticking your finger in a glass of water to see if it's hot or cold. You put a tiny part of yourself into the vessel, and when you bring it back out, you've gained all the experiences it had.

"You've been a human for the last 48 years, so you haven't stretched out yet and felt the rest of your immense consciousness. If we hung out here for long enough, you'd start remembering everything. But there's no point in doing that between each life."

"How many times have I been reincarnated, then?"

"Oh lots. Lots and lots. And into lots of different lives." I said. "This time around, you'll be a Chinese peasant girl in 540 AD."

"Wait, what?" You stammered. "You're sending me back in time?"

"Well, I guess technically. Time, as you know it, only exists in your universe. Things are different where I come from."

"Where do You come from?" You said.

"Oh sure," I explained, "I come from somewhere. Somewhere else. And there are others like me. I know you'll want to know what it's like there, but honestly, you wouldn't understand."

"Oh," you said, a little let down. "But wait. If I get reincarnated to other places in time, I could have interacted with myself at some point."

"Sure. Happens all the time. And with both lives only aware of their own lifespan, you don't even know it's happening."

"So, what's the point of it all?"

"Seriously?" I asked. "Seriously? You're asking Me for the meaning of life? Isn't that a little stereotypical?"

"Well, it's a reasonable question," you persisted.

I looked you in the eye. "The meaning of life, the reason I made this whole universe, is for you to mature."

"You mean mankind? You want us to mature?"

"No, just you. I made this whole universe for you. With each new life you grow and mature and become a larger and greater intellect."

"Just me? What about everyone else?"

"There is no one else," I said. "In this universe, there's just you and Me."

You stared blankly at Me. "But all the people on earth…"

"All you. Different incarnations of you."

"Wait. I'm *everyone*!?"

"Now you're getting it," I said, with a congratulatory slap on the back.

"I'm every human being who ever lived?"

"Or who will ever live, yes."

"I'm Abraham Lincoln?"

"And you're John Wilkes Booth, too," I added.

"I'm Hitler?" You said, appalled.

"And you're the millions he killed."

"I'm Jesus?"

"And you're everyone who followed him."

You fell silent.

"Every time you victimized someone," I said, "you were victimizing yourself. Every act of kindness you've done, you've done to yourself. Every happy and sad moment ever experienced by any human was, or will be, experienced by you."

You thought for a long time.

"Why?" You asked Me. "Why do all this?"

"Because someday, you will become like Me. Because that's what you *are*. You're one of My kind. You're My child."

"Whoa," you said, incredulous. "You mean I'm a God?"

"No. Not yet. You're a fetus. You're still growing. Once you've lived every human life throughout all time, you will have grown enough to be born."

"So the whole universe," you said, "it's just…"

"An egg." I answered. "Now it's time for you to move on to your next life."

And I sent you on your way.

## Microsoft Bing's Summary

The Egg by Andy Weir is a thought-provoking short story about a man who dies and meets God. In the story, the man learns that he has been reincarnated many times before and that all human beings who have ever lived and will ever live are incarnations of Him. God explains that the entire universe was created as an egg for the main character, all of humanity, and once he has lived every human life ever, he will be born as a Christ. The story explores the idea that every time you victimize someone, you are victimizing yourself and that every act of kindness you do, you do to yourself. Every happy and sad moment ever experienced by any human was or will be experienced by you. The idea is that we are all connected and that our actions have consequences not only for others but also for ourselves. The man is surprised to learn that he has been everyone from Abraham Lincoln to Adolf Hitler. The man is next to be reincarnated as a Chinese peasant girl in 540 AD. One of the main themes is the Oneness of all human beings. The story suggests that every person who has ever lived and will ever live is an incarnation of the same *Being*. This means that every action we take has consequences not only for others, but also for ourselves. This realization leads him to understand the importance of treating others with kindness and compassion.

The fictional short story "The Egg" by Andy Weir presents a perspective on existence that aligns with certain spiritual teachings, including ACIM. The story suggests that every person who has ever lived or will ever live is an incarnation of the same Being, experiencing life through different perspectives to ultimately achieve enlightenment. An egg serves as a protective environment for an embryo, allowing it to grow until it is ready to be born into life. Similarly, this illusory universe was created as a refuge from God. However, when the mind listens to the Holy Spirit, the universe's purpose shifts, it becomes an Egg that shelters God's Son until

He is ready to awaken to His true nature as a Christ Being. The idea of reincarnation, as referenced in "The Egg", suggests that each life script is written for the purpose of learning and refining the soul's understanding. Lessons learned in previous lives purify the subconscious, ensuring they do not need to be repeated. The ultimate goal is achieving perfection in forgiveness. The perception of historical figures, such as Adolf Hitler, is always filtered through personal and societal narratives. The Holy Spirit's Divine knowledge reveals the truth beyond human judgment, a mind writing its own script to ultimately attain the miraculous ability to forgive completely. In essence, "The Egg" can be seen as non-fiction in the sense that each illusory life serves a singular purpose: the remembrance that we are Christ, God's first creation. The story's message reinforces the idea that every action, whether kindness or harm, is ultimately experienced by the same Being. "Every time you victimized someone," I said, "you were victimizing yourself. Every act of kindness you've done, you've done to yourself. Every happy and sad moment ever experienced by any human was, or will be, experienced by you." "Why?" You asked Me. "Why do all this?" "Because someday, you will become like Me. Because that's what you are. You're one of My kind. You're My Child." This perspective invites reflection on the interconnectedness of all existence and the journey toward divine remembrance. Bob

CHAPTER 37

# Questions For Artificial Intelligence

I asked Artificial Intelligence some questions about "The Bible", "A Course In Miracles" and "Disappearance" Of The Universe". I used the Microsoft Bing Search Engine. You'll find the answers very interesting. I know I have.

Q. Who wrote the Bible and why?

A. The Bible is a collection of 66 books written by multiple authors over a period of time. The Old Testament, or Hebrew Bible, narrates the history of the people of Israel over about a millennium, beginning with God's creation of the world and humankind. It contains the stories, laws, and moral lessons that form the basis of religious life for both Jews and Christians. For at least 1,000 years, both Jewish and Christian traditions held that a single author wrote the first five books of the Bible, Genesis, Exodus, Leviticus, Numbers, and Deuteronomy, which together are known as the Torah (Hebrew for "instruction") and the Pentateuch (Greek for "five scrolls"). That single author was believed to be Moses, the Hebrew prophet who led the Israelites out of captivity in Egypt and guided them across the Red Sea toward the Promised Land. However, there are things in these books that Moses himself could not possibly have witnessed: His own death, for example, occurs near the end of Deuteronomy. A volume of the Talmud dealt with this inconsistency by explaining that Joshua (Moses' successor as leader of the Israelites) likely wrote the verses about Moses' death.

The New Testament was written by multiple authors including Matthew, Mark, Luke, John, Paul, James, Peter, and Jude. These books were written to spread the teachings of Jesus Christ and to provide guidance to early Christian communities. The Bible is considered to be Divinely inspired by many believers. Some believe that God wrote the Bible through human authors. They actually held the quill that moved across the parchment, but what they wrote was ultimately what God wanted to be written.

Q. Who wrote ACIM and why?

A. "A Course In Miracles" (ACIM) is a 1976 book that was scribed by Helen Schucman between 1965 and 1972 through a process of inner dictation. Schucman said that the book had been dictated to her, word for word, via a process of "inner dictation" from Jesus Christ. The underlying premise of the book is that the greatest "miracle" is the act of simply gaining a full "awareness of Love's presence" in a person's life.

Q. Is The Bible all true?

A. Whether the Bible is all true is a complex one, and opinions on the matter vary. Some people believe that the Bible is the literal word of God and that everything in it is true. Others believe that while the Bible contains important spiritual truths, it should not be taken as a literal historical or scientific account. Still, others believe that the Bible is a human creation and that its contents are not necessarily true.

Q. Is ACIM all true?

A. Whether ACIM is all true is a complex one, and opinions on the matter vary. ACIM is a 1976 book by Helen Schucman. Again, the underlying premise is that the greatest "miracle" is the act of simply gaining a full "awareness of Love's presence" in a person's life. Schucman said that the book had been dictated to her, word for word, via a process of "inner dictation" from Jesus Christ. Some people believe that ACIM contains essential spiritual truths.

Q. What is the difference between the God of the Bible and the God of ACIM?

A. The God of the Bible and the God of ACIM are understood differently by different people. ACIM is a book by Helen Schucman that was published in 1976. According to her testimony, Schucman began having "highly symbolic dreams" and experiencing "strange images." As she began to write, she was surprised to see "This is

ACIM" appear on the paper. She went on to say that this was her introduction to the "Voice." This voice began to give her rapid inner dictation that she took down in shorthand. According to the dictated material, the voice of The Course was Jesus. On the other hand, the God of the Bible is understood by many as the creator of the universe and everything in it. The Bible contains accounts of God's interactions with humanity, including His miracles, commandments, and promises.

Q. According to the Bible, can God be jealous, vindictive, and cruel?

A. According to the Bible, God is described as having a range of emotions, including jealousy. In Exodus 20:5, God says, "You shall not bow down to them or serve them, for I the Lord your God am a jealous God." However, it's significant to note that the concept of jealousy in this context is different from the human emotion of jealousy. God's jealousy is often understood as righteous jealousy for His people, whom He Loves and wants to protect from harm. The Bible also contains passages where God is described as punishing those who disobey Him. However, many people believe that these actions are not vindictive or cruel, but rather are just and necessary consequences for disobedience. It's essential to note that interpretations of the Bible can vary, and different people may have different understandings of these passages.

Q. According to ACIM can God be jealous, vindictive, and cruel?

A. According to ACIM, God is not capable of being jealous, vindictive, or cruel. ACIM teaches that God is Love and that His nature is only Loving. The book presents a view of God as a Loving creator who does not punish or condemn His creations. Instead, ACIM teaches that any perception of punishment or cruelty is a result of our own mistaken beliefs and not a reflection of God's true nature.

Q. Does the Bible mention Satan and hell?

A. Yes, the Bible does mention Satan and hell. According to the Bible, hell was originally designed for Satan and his demons. The Bible also states that hell will punish the sin of those who reject Christ. hell is described as a place of conscious torment, with references such as "furnace of fire, weeping and gnashing of teeth" (Matthew 13:50), "where their worm does not die, and the fire is not quenched" (Mark 9:48), and "he will be tormented with fire and brimstone" (Revelation 14:10). The Bible also refers to hell as a place of everlasting fire prepared for the Devil and his angels. However, it does not state that the devil will reign over hell, just that he will eventually be banished there.

Q. If hell is real, how can the Bible state that God is Love?

A. This is a complex question that has been debated by theologians and scholars for centuries. There are many interpretations and opinions on this topic. Some people believe that God's Love and the existence of hell are not contradictory. They argue that God is Loving, but also just, and that hell is a place of punishment for those who reject God's Love and choose to live in sin. Others believe that the idea of eternal torment is repugnant to God and contrary to the Bible's teaching that "God is Love". There are also those who believe that hell is simply the final result of a human being saying to God throughout life, "Go away and leave me alone." hell is God's answer, "You may have your wish." In that sense, hell is the ultimate testament to human freedom.

Q. Do some Biblical scholars say hell was made up to scare society, keep them in line, and have them give money to the church?

A. Yes, some Biblical scholars and historians argue that the concept of hell as a place of eternal punishment was created by the early Christian church to scare people into obedience and to increase the church's power and wealth. They believe that the idea of hell as a place of eternal torment was not part of the original teachings of Jesus or the early Christian church, but was added later as a means of control.

Q. According to ACIM do Satan and hell exist?

A. ACIM asserts that there is no hell. It considers hell to be a projection of our own guilt and a figment of our tormented imagination. Essentially, it challenges the traditional concept of hell. ACIM does not want us to believe in Satan. Instead, it encourages a personal relationship with God and views Jesus as the way to the Father. It does not promote idolatry or false worship.

Q. According to the Bible, what is ego?

A. The term ego is not explicitly mentioned in the Bible. However, the concept of ego, or the self, is addressed in various passages. In the

Bible, the self is often portrayed as something that needs to be denied or put to death in order to follow Christ and live a life pleasing to God. For example, in Matthew 16:24, Jesus says "If anyone desires to come after Me, let him deny himself, and take up his cross, and follow Me". In Galatians 2:20, Paul writes "I have been crucified with Christ; it is no longer I who live, but Christ lives in me; and the life which I Now live in the flesh I live by faith in the Son of God, who Loved me and gave Himself for me".

Q. According to ACIM, what is ego?

A. According to ACIM, the ego is the idea of separation from God, and it is the source of all fear and guilt. The ego is described as a false self, created by the mind as a defense against the fear of losing its identity. The ego is seen as the cause of all conflict and suffering, and its thought system is based on attack and defense. The Course teaches that the ego can be undone by recognizing its unreality and choosing to listen to the voice of the Holy Spirit instead, which leads to the experience of peace and Love.

Q. According to the Bible, why did God make Christ?

A. According to the Bible, God sent Jesus, his one and only Son, to live as a man for several reasons. One reason is to demonstrate God's Love for humanity. In Romans 5:6–8, Paul writes, "For while we were still weak, at the right time Christ died for the ungodly. For one will scarcely die for a righteous person, though perhaps for a good person one would dare even to die, but God shows his Love for us in that while we were still sinners, Christ died for us". Another reason is to restore the fullness of God's image in humanity. Because of our sin, we have fallen short of reflecting God's glory as we should. Therefore, God sent his son Jesus as "the image of the invisible God, the firstborn over all creation". Through his life of perfect obedience, his sacrificial death on the cross for our sins, and his resurrection from the dead, Jesus begins to restore the fullness of God's image in us.

Q. According to ACIM, why did God make Christ?

A. According to ACIM, God created Christ as an extension of His very nature. ACIM teaches that God is Love and that His creations, including Christ, are created in His likeness, thus extending His nature of Love.

Q. According to the Bible, is it possible to sin against God?

A. Yes, most certainly it is very possible. According to the Bible, sin is a transgression of God's law. It involves violating God's prohibitive commands or omitting to practice His positive commands. Since God's law reflects His holy nature, any act of sin is ultimately against Him personally. In other words, sin is an offense directed toward God, whether through disobedience, rebellion, or other wrongful actions.

Q. According to ACIM is it possible to sin against God?

A. In ACIM, sin is described as insanity, a means by which the mind becomes mad and seeks to replace truth with illusions. It perceives illusions where truth should be. Sin gave rise to the body's senses, but the sinless have no need for sights, sounds, or touch. To sense is not to know; truth is filled with knowledge alone. Illusions, born from untrue thoughts, serve as "proof" that what lacks Reality is real. Sin falsely claims that God's Son is evil, that timelessness must end, and eternal life can die. Yet, God's Love remains unchanging, even amidst our pretenses. So, how long will we maintain this game of sin?

Q. Jesus explains in ACIM that God sees no sin in us because we're merely dreaming. Is this true?

A. In ACIM the concept of sin is indeed approached from a unique perspective. According to ACIM, our earthly existence is like a dream, a projection of illusions that veil our true nature. In this dream, we perceive separation, guilt, and fear, leading to what we call sin. However, God, being all-knowing and loving, sees beyond the dream. To Him, our perceived sins are like fleeting shadows in a play. They hold no ultimate Reality because our True Essence remains sinless and eternal . *So, yes, from the perspective of Divine Truth, sin is an illusion, a temporary distortion of our inherent holiness.*

Q. According to The Bible, who is Jesus?

A. According to the Bible, Jesus is the Son of God, equal with God, and with authority from the Father. In Luke 22:70, it is written, "Then they all said, are You then the Son of God?' So He said to them, 'You rightly say that I am'". In Matthew 28:18, Jesus says, "All authority has been given to Me in heaven and on earth". In John 5:17, it is written "Therefore the Jews sought all the more to kill Him because He not only broke the Sabbath but also said that God was His Father, making Himself equal with God". Jesus is also referred to as the Christ, the Messiah, and the Anointed One.

Q. According to ACIM, who is Jesus?

A. According to ACIM, Jesus is the name of one who was a man but saw the face of Christ in all his brothers and remembered God. So he became identified with Christ, a man no longer, but at One with God. The man was an illusion, for he seemed to be a separate being, walking by himself, within a body that appeared to hold himself from Self, as all illusions do. Yet who can save unless he sees illusions and then identifies them for what they are? Jesus remains a Savior because he saw the false without accepting it as true. And Christ needed his form so that He might appear to men and save them from their own illusions.

Q. According to the Bible, who is the Holy Spirit?

A. According to the Bible, the Holy Spirit is the third person of the Trinity, along with God the Father and God the Son (Jesus Christ). The Holy Spirit is a person, not an impersonal force or influence. He has personal attributes such as intelligence, emotions, and will. He teaches, commands, and intercedes for us in prayer. The Holy Spirit is also referred to as the Advocate, the Spirit of truth, and the Comforter.

Q. According to ACIM, who is the Holy Spirit?

A. According to ACIM, the Holy Spirit is a mediator between illusions and the truth. She must bridge the gap between Reality and dreams, and perception leads to knowledge through the grace that God has given Her, to be His gift to everyone who turns to Him for truth. Across the bridge that She provides, dreams are carried to the truth, to be dispelled before the light of knowledge. The goal of the Holy Spirit's teaching is just this end of dreams. For sights and sounds must be translated from the witnesses of fear to those of Love. And when this is entirely accomplished, learning has achieved the only goal it has in Truth. For learning, as the Holy Spirit guides it to the outcome She perceives for it, becomes the means to go beyond itself, to be replaced by the Eternal Truth.

Q. According to the Bible, did God create the universe?

A. According to the Bible, God created the universe. In the Book of Genesis, it says, "In the beginning, when God created the universe, the earth was formless and desolate." The process of creation unfolds over several days, with God separating light from darkness, creating the sky, land, plants, animals, and finally, human beings. Additionally, Colossians 1:16 affirms that all things were created through God and for Him.

Q. According to ACIM, did God create the universe?

A. According to ACIM, the physical universe (including the body) was not created by God, and in fact, came about as an attempt to hide from God due to intense fear.

Q. According to ACIM can our perfect God make anything or anyone imperfect?

A. ACIM presents a unique perspective on God and creation. It suggests that God is perfect and unchanging, and therefore cannot create imperfection. In ACIM, the material world, including our bodies and egos, is considered illusory, a projection of the ego's fear and separation from God. From this viewpoint, imperfections arise from our misperceptions and identification with the ego, not from any inherent flaw in God's creation. ACIM teaches that our True Nature is beyond the physical realm, and our journey involves awakening to this Truth and releasing illusions.

Q. ACIM says we're dreaming, and this universe is not real, why did we start dreaming?

A. According to ACIM, the dream of separation and the physical universe came about as a result of a tiny, mad idea that seemed to enter the mind of the Son of God. This idea was the thought of separation from God, and it seemed to cause a split in the mind of the Son of God, leading to the projection of a world of multiplicity and separation. The Course teaches that this dream is not real and has no effect on our true Reality, which is eternal and changeless. We can awaken from this dream by practicing forgiveness and changing our perception of the world.

Q. In "Disappearance Of The Universe" by Gary Renard it claims that God was asked a question by Christ that was not answered. What was the question?

A. I'm sorry, but I couldn't find any specific information about a question that Christ asked God that was not answered.

Q. In "Disappearance Of The Universe", what does pg.123 state?

A. I'm sorry, but I don't have the ability to access specific pages of books. I can only provide general information about the book and its contents.

Q. Pg.123 states for a nanosecond a small aspect of Christ appears to have an idea that was not shared by God. The question was like, "What would it be like to go off and play on my own?" Which unfortunately is followed by an apparent answer. What was God's Answer?

A. I'm sorry, but I couldn't find any specific information about God's answer to the question, "What would it be like to go off and play on my own?"

Q. In "Disappearance Of The Universe", it says God did not answer the question because the idea was not of God. Therefore, was God's answer not answering?

A. According to "The Disappearance Of The Universe" by Gary Renard, it is stated that God did not answer the question because the idea was not of God. In this context, it could be interpreted that God's answer was not answering.

Q. Were there Sons of God before the dream of separation?

A. According to ACIM, before the dream of separation, there was only the Son of God, who is One with God and is an extension of God's perfect Love and Oneness. The Son of God is often referred to in the plural as the "Sons of God" to represent the idea that all of us are part of the one Sonship. Before the dream of separation, the Sons of God existed in a state of perfect Oneness with God and with each other.

Q. Therefore, before the dream of separation there were separate personalities of the One Christ Mind?

A. According to ACIM, before the dream of separation, there was only the Son of God, who is One with God and is an extension of God's perfect Love and Oneness. Before the dream of separation, the Sons of God existed in a state of perfect Oneness with God and with each other. In this state, there were no separate personalities or individual identities, but rather a perfect unity and harmony within the one Christ Mind.

Q. So therefore the Sons of God occurred inside the dream of separation?

A. According to ACIM, the dream of separation is an illusion that seems to have occurred within the mind of the Son of God. In this dream, the one Sonship appears to have fragmented into many individuals, or "Sons of God," each with their own separate identity and personality. However, the Course teaches that this separation is not real and has no effect on our true Reality, which is eternal and changeless.

Q. Clarify the statement the dream of separation is an illusion that seems to have occurred within the Mind of the Son of God.

A. This means that the separation from God and the fragmentation of the One Sonship into many individuals is not real, but rather an illusory dream that seems to have taken place within the mind of the Son of God.

Q. According to both books, will we see and know our Loved ones who died in our dream when we awaken in Heaven?

A. According to ACIM, when we awaken from the dream of separation and return to the awareness of our Oneness with God, we will experience a state of perfect Love and unity with all beings. In this state, the individual personalities and identities that we associate with our Loved ones will no longer be relevant, as we will all be united in the One Christ Mind. However, the Love that we share with our Loved ones will continue to exist and will be experienced in a more profound and complete way.

Q. So therefore in Heaven we will retain the different personalities and memories we developed in our dream, but all will be purified because we realize we are all One in the Mind Of Christ?

A. The memories and experiences that we have accumulated in the dream of separation will be seen in a new light, as we realize that they were part of an illusory dream and have no effect on our true Reality. In this sense, our personalities and memories will be purified as we awaken to the Truth of our Oneness with God and with each other.

Q. So therefore the Love we share with our Loved ones means our Loved ones are there as we remember them from our dream?

A. While the specific details of our individual personalities and identities may no longer be relevant in this state of perfect unity, the Love that we share with our Loved ones will continue to exist. It will be experienced in a deeper and more meaningful way. The focus shifts from the individual details of our personalities to the underlying Love and connection that we share with all beings. So, while we may not remember our Loved ones exactly as they were in our dream of separation, the essence of our connection with them, the Love we share, will continue to exist in a more profound and complete way.

Q. When we awaken from our dream of separation, will we retain our memories?

A. The question whether we will retain our memories when we awaken from our dream of separation is a complex one, and opinions on the matter vary. According to ACIM it's possible that our memories and experiences in the dream of separation may be transformed or transcended as we awaken to a greater awareness of our true nature as spiritual beings.

Q. According to ACIM and "Disappearance", were all animals and sea creatures created in Heaven or in our dream?

A. According to ACIM and "Disappearance", the idea of separation from God is an illusion. ACIM teaches that the physical world, including all animals and sea creatures, is part of this illusion and not real in the ultimate sense.

Q. Since we retain our memories in Heaven and will be Co-Creators with God, is it possible that we'll be able to create all animals and sea creatures to inhabit Heaven?

A. The question whether we will be able to create all animals and sea creatures to inhabit Heaven is a complex one, and opinions on the matter vary. It's possible that our understanding of creation and our role as Co-Creators with God may be transformed or transcended as we awaken to a greater awareness of our True Nature as spiritual beings.

Q. In ACIM or "Disappearance" does it say when we wake up that we will know *all* God knows, being that we are One with Christ and Christ is One with God?

A. Neither ACIM nor "Disappearance" specifically addresses the question whether we will know all that God knows when we awaken from the dream of separation.

Q. In "Disappearance" which is in alignment with ACIM how could Arten and Pursha just appear and disappear? Is it possible they learned this in Heaven?

A. It's possible that Arten and Pursah's ability to appear and disappear is a reflection of their spiritual nature and their understanding of the illusory nature of the physical world.

Q. Jesus states in ACIM that every action we performed in our dream due to Love will be purified by him and offered as gifts. What does this mean?

A. This statement reflects a profound spiritual perspective. Let's break it down. Dream and Reality: ACIM teaches that our earthly existence is like a dream, an illusion. Our actions within this dream are not ultimately real. Love, however, is considered a higher truth, a reflection of our Divine nature. Purification: When we act from a place of Love, genuine compassion, kindness, and selflessness, those actions are seen as pure. Jesus, as a symbol of Divine Love and forgiveness in ACIM, purifies these loving actions. This means he transforms them beyond their illusory nature. Offering as Gifts: The purified actions are then offered as gifts to God or the higher Self. In this context, God represents the ultimate Reality, beyond the dream. These gifts symbolize our willingness to transcend ego-based actions and align with Love. Transcending Illusion: By recognizing the illusory nature of our actions and choosing Love, we move closer to awakening from the dream. The gifts we offer become a pathway to awakening, a way to remember our true identity. ACIM invites us to question our perceptions, release grievances, and select Love over fear. Ultimately, it encourages us to awaken from the dream of separation and recognize our Oneness with God.

Q. Is it possible the term Christ is a State of Being? ACIM declares the extreme importance of forgiving. In other words, if we obtain perfection in forgiveness, we will awaken to the Truth that we are a Christ Being and not a human being.

A. In ACIM the term Christ holds a profound and transformative meaning. Let's explore it further: The Christ State of Being: According to ACIM, the Christ is not merely a historical figure (such as Jesus) but a universal state of consciousness. It represents our true identity beyond the limitations of the ego and the physical body. The Christ state of being is characterized by Love, forgiveness, and Oneness with God. It transcends the illusion of separation and recognizes the Divine essence in all beings. It's the living expression of Light within us, a recognition that we are interconnected, eternal , and part of a greater whole. Forgiveness and Awakening: ACIM emphasizes forgiveness as a central practice. By forgiving ourselves and others, we release the ego's grip on our minds and open ourselves to the Christ consciousness. When we forgive, we let go of grievances, judgments, and illusions. In this process, we awaken to our true nature, the Christ within us. Forgiveness is not about condoning harmful actions; it's about recognizing that everyone is worthy of Love and redemption, regardless of their past behavior. Beyond human identity: As you mentioned, when we attain perfection in forgiveness, we move beyond the limited perception of being a mere human being. We recognize our Divine origin. The Christ within us is not bound by time, space, or physical form. It is eternal , unchanging, and connected to the Source. In this state, we see through the illusion of separateness and experience unity with all creation. Remember that ACIM invites us to practice forgiveness daily, allowing the Christ consciousness to shine through our interactions and perceptions. It's a journey toward awakening, a shift from human identity to Divine realization.

In summary, this is Divine Truth from Jesus and the Holy Spirit. In Heaven, we will no longer carry the burden of the ego. Our minds will be fully active, unhindered by limitation. As expressed in the words, "Knock, and the door shall be opened; ask, and ye shall receive," this truth remains eternal. Upon awakening, we probably will not instantly know all that God knows. Yet, if one seeks understanding, such as how to create a universe, they will be taught. Ultimately, we will arrive at the magnificent realization that we are Co-Creators with God. This is the essence of Truth, for God's very nature is to share His Being with creation. It is vital to recognize that we are not merely human beings, we are Christ Beings.

CHAPTER 38

# Lana's Writings

THE FOLLOWING WRITINGS COME from my Facebook friend, Lana. She's 75 and is one of the most gifted authors I know. Lana explained, "About eight years ago, I was diagnosed with a terminal illness, Pulmonary Fibrosis. There was no cure nor even treatment. The doctors told me that in an otherwise healthy person, which I was not, the outlook was that I had about a year to live. However, deep within my Heart, it did not seem real to me. I went into meditation and asked Jesus,"What is the truth of this?" His response was so comforting. Jesus told me, "Let the doctors take care of your body and I will take care of your mind." *Knowing that the mind was the only thing that could truly be sick,* I depended on Jesus to keep my mind healed, and I had an *inner knowing* that as an effect of a healed mind, my body would also be healed. The next few months were a real adventure and a test of trusting that truth was True. I did let the doctors, I had three, take care of my body but paid little attention to what transpired because I was focused with Jesus on keeping my mind healed and *open to receive miracles.* Over the next six months, my MRI's painted a picture of healing which left my doctors puzzled and confused. At first, they thought I just had a slowly progressing type of Pulmonary Fibrosis. Then, the progression of my illness seemed to stop entirely. Finally, the scar tissue that had been growing in my lungs began to disappear. Again this left my doctors scratching their heads in bewilderment, wondering how this could be possible. I knew how it was possible and just watched my healing unfold, as my trust in God grew stronger and stronger.

    This is just one of the many healing miracles I've experienced over the years. One so-called body adventure took me to death's door as I was given the last rites of the Church. I have written about my NDE and its miraculous nature that took me beyond my body into another spatial dimension where I was filled with the peace and joy of God. It was given me realize that it was perfectly OK to stay in my body or to leave it. It was my choice. On another occasion, I experienced two heart attacks within a few hours and had to be flown to a hospital that was better equipped to handle my situation. During the trip, I was floating above my body and was able to watch the medical attendant try to keep me alive until we arrived at the hospital in Boston. During this time, I felt no pain and was in a state of perfect peace. Once again, I felt it was perfectly fine to return to my body or leave it behind. Both times, I felt perfectly safe and protected and had no fear at all. I no longer fear body adventures or even the demise of the body. Whenever they occur and for whatever reason they occur, I simply keep my Heart and mind fixed on God and surrender myself to the Will of God. I just summit, "Let it be done unto me according to Thy Will." These are the same words spoken by the Blessed Mother when she was told she would be the mother of Jesus. There were other times as well, but the ones mentioned above brought the greatest lessons to me. What I learned was that there is *absolutely nothing to fear.* Just beyond the shadow of the valley of death, there is something else that clicks in and takes over. I've only experienced this something else during the two NDE's mentioned above. This something else just took over my entire being, providing the assurance that everything was as it should be and that everything would be OK. I trusted it completely and just went along for the ride, it was a miraculous and beautiful spiritual ride." The next articles were written while she was recovering. Her writings are true and astounding.

## Part 1: When the path to hell transforms into the path to Heaven.

The following essay comes in three parts. That's just how Jesus announced it to me in this morning's meditative writing. The next part will come within the next day or two, it usually does. This part begins a little dark, but then becomes bright and shiny by the end. So here it goes, when the path to hell transforms into the path to Heaven. By Now at least for most of us we have tested out forgiveness and experienced its healing effects. No longer is it an abstract concept, but a living and known fact based on our actual experience. Most of us know the drill by Now. It often plays out as a journey into hell and then back to Heaven again. First, we notice we are not at peace, or we notice the symptoms of losing our peace. We may think, "Oh no, here it comes." There are so many symptoms, and we can experience one or many of them. There is anxiety or worry present. Pain, either physical or emotional, shows up. Or, we notice we are stuck in what seems to be an unsolvable problem. In general, we feel lethargic, unmotivated, and maybe even depressed. Perhaps there is a grievance or anger present towards someone or something. For whatever reason, we feel we are lacking something that if found would solve everything and return us to wholeness, completion, and to peace. There are other symptoms too numerous to mention. These "appearances" tell us that our mind seems to have been taken over by some alien power that Jesus in ACIM refers to as "ego." It is a nothing, appearing as something, and it seems to have captured us as its prisoner. It feels so real and so much a part of us that we misidentify it as being us. It can feel like we are possessed or hypnotized by some unknown force. It makes us feel alone, separated and abandoned by God. The voice of the ego frightens us and keeps us in a state of fear. We may even come to believe the only way to survive is to bow to its will instead of the Will of God. The voice of the ego always comes gift-wrapped in specific stories or situations that seem to validate its lies and convince us that they must be true. These stories and situations are but effects of the ego mentality and only serve to keep us under the ego's grip and control. There then comes an endless process of seek but do not find, for there are no answers in the ego's grab bag, which is based solely on the past. The past is the only point of reference the ego has as a source for any and all information. Yet, like the ego, there is no past and there is no time. Nothing the ego offers us has a thread of truth within it. Yet, as unbelievable as it seems, while under the spell of the ego, there seems to be logic. Granted, it is a sick, distorted logic based on the ego's misperceptions and lies and only makes sense to a sick mind under its influence. Is any of this starting to sound familiar? The voice of the ego takes us on a journey towards hell. We become time travelers. It keeps our mind fixed and focused on past regrets and future worries. It is the complete opposite of the Voice of God, which leads us on the path to Heaven. Its path is a peaceful one and can only be found here and Now. The Voice for God does not time-travel but, rather, keeps our focus on *Now*. What Jesus teaches us is the closest approximation we have in our human experience to eternity , and leads us to our true Home in God. I don't think a day goes by that I don't thank God for "A

Course In Miracles". It is an out-of-time communication brought to us in time because that is where we believe we are, and God always meets us where we are, or we believe we are. Jesus, in ACIM, comes to remind us that spells can be broken and that there is a remedy for ego's spell as well. ACIM reminds me that everything that is true and real is also eternal. Its everlasting and unchanging nature is still present within the mind I share with God. It reminds me that every loving thought I've ever had is saved for me for all eternity. All I need to do is touch the hem of God's Love, right here and right Now, and the ego's spell is broken. Anything and everything touched by Love's presence is healed, restored, and returned to peace. We remember and recognize that our God-given free will is still intact, and we can always *choose once again.*

The one solution for any and all perceived problems is simply in our decision to return the mind to God, right here and right Now. It comes through our willingness to forgive what never was. It comes with the willingness to accept the Atonement for ourselves. Willingness is the key. The willingness to see things differently, willingness to be here Now, willingness to allow forgiveness to heal, willingness to be healed, willingness to accept God's Will instead of an alien will separate from God's. The willingness to return to the path to Heaven, and to peace. Willingness to join in unity with God and all of our brothers. The rewards are infinite. Most cannot be expressed through the word symbols of any language, but I do *know* this. With the healing of the mind comes everything I could ever want or desire. It comes with clarity, certainty, and peace. I recognize, I realize, and I remember who I am, who my brothers are, and who God Is. For me, the entire process I feel is summed up in one sentence, "Love recognizes Love and remembers Itself." Also, there are two scripture verses that have miraculously come alive within me. No longer just flowery words, they live within me as absolute truth. "God is Love, and he that abides in Love abides in God and God in him." The second one is, "My Father and I are One." Jesus tells us that ACIM is a beginning, not an end. Its goal is to know Thyself. Now that we are aware of who we truly are, and Now that we are awake to the fact that we are dreaming, Jesus is still here to guide us in how to navigate through this human experience. He did this over 2,000 years ago. To be in the world but not of the world, and to practice forgiveness in every situation. Or, as Wayne Dyer always said, to function as Spirit having a human experience. Jesus has a lot to say about all of this.

## Part 2: When the path to hell transforms into the path to Heaven.

Let us continue in our transition from the path to hell to Heaven's way. Part two may begin as a little too metaphysical for some, but it is fundamental. It is fundamental in our understanding of how the path to Heaven is wide open and available to all of us to choose. Its password is Love. Being it, extending it, sharing it, demonstrating it, and living it. We are really not going anywhere that Love is not. It just appears that way through distorted perception. The means of healing these distortions is *forgiveness*, the motivation is inner peace, and the goal is, know Thyself. The return to Heaven's path is the return to Love's awareness. Since in truth, Heaven is a state of mind, the path to Heaven begins in the mind. Heaven has never left our mind, and we have never left Heaven. Yet, perceiving via a split mind can make the path confusing. It is important to remember we are Spirit first and always. Yet, within our dream-like existence, we seem to be having a human experience. Just as the goal of ACIM is to know Thyself, so is it that we transform the path to hell into the path to Heaven by knowing Thyself. It comes from the power of knowing our Real, True, and eternal Self, as God created us. Jesus tells us. "The term mind is used to represent the activating agent of spirit, supplying its creative energy." I find this whole section so significant in our acceptance of *who we truly are*. How our perception of it being split between Spirit and ego can really mess up our discernment of what is real and what is not. The fact that the mind is the activating agent of the Spirit is key. Yet, because of its split nature, the mind can be misused on behalf of the ego, but only if there is a belief in place that this so-called ego is a real thing. Our perceptions follow the beliefs that are embedded within the mind. Our beliefs are projected out and perceived as real. Projection makes perception. We can never depend on our perceptions to tell us anything of truth. They distort and hide the truth about everything we see. So we see nothing as it actually is. Mind can only act as it is directed. It will either respond to Love and activate Spirit, or it will react to fear and seem to activate ego. The first is a *real* response and the latter is an imagined reaction, believed to be real. It all comes down to Who/what is in control of the mind at any given moment. Love or fear. We are called to look within and ask, "Am I functioning from my right mind (Holy Spirit) or my wrong mind (ego)?" and, "At this moment, is my mind aligned with truth or illusion?" The real question is, "Am I at peace?" That answer tells me everything I need to know.

It is why keeping a present state of awareness is so critical to maintaining a peaceful experience of life. Am I at peace? Even asking this question will automatically bring your focus and attention back to *Now*. This is because the answer can only be found within us, right here and right Now. And, you will get an immediate answer, *for only you know if you are at peace*. You can't get the answer from anywhere outside yourself, only by looking directly within. The bottom line is that if I am not at peace, I am not in my right mind. If I am not in my right mind, then my mind must be aligned with fear. And if I go ahead and react while in this state of mind, it is by my decision the ego is activated instead of Spirit. We all know how the effects of that decision will play out in our experience. Here and Now is where this decision is made because in truth there is no other place or time that exists. Yet, that fact is not helpful to us if our awareness is off traveling in time and engaging past regrets or future worries. It is our awareness that must be present, our conscious awareness, so we can make conscious choices. Otherwise, the choice is made for us and is seldom the right-minded one because it is based on our established and habitual pattern of thinking. Usually, if not always, it is controlled by the thought system of the ego. It is an imaginary thought system, but one that is believed to be real. This moment of decision between responding with Love or reacting with fear is not a time to think. It is the time to *trust*. It is the means to rule the Kingdom of our mind and to direct the mind to activate the Spirit of God within, the mind we all share in Unity as One with our beloved Creator.

This is what training the mind means, and how it relates to the quality and peace of our everyday life. To not maintain a present state of awareness, is like relinquishing our freedom and our power as the Son of God. You can never lose it, but if it is out of our awareness, what good can it do for us? Here/Now is the mission control center of the mind. Our mind-training helps reprogram our thinking to stay alert to the condition of the mind. The more we check in, the more we begin to notice the first hints of discomfort. At that moment, we are present to make the choice for God, thereby activating the Spirit and Creative Power of God within us. At that moment of making the conscious and deliberate decision to choose God, the Spirit is activated, It steps in, and takes care of everything *for* us. In that instant, all thinking stops. The mind can relax and rest in God, knowing that whatever is in need of healing will be healed, and most likely the only thing in need of healing is itself, the mind.

If you noticed, there was nothing for you to understand. There was nothing for you to fix or figure out. There was nothing for you to even think about. There was nothing for you to do, *but* trust in God and in truth being True. We act on it by making the right choice for God/Love. With this decision, the mind was healed, returned to right-minded perception, and you returned to peace. Always remember Divine Order. First comes forgiveness and healing. With the healing of the mind comes understanding, clarity, certainty, and the Peace of God. In the process, we are also learning not to confuse cause and effect. In truth, there is no gap between them, just as there is no gap in giving/receiving. But perceptually, they do seem to play out linearly, a first this and then that experience. For the purpose of forgiveness, the cause of any misperception is the mind, and the effects of the misperception show up in our experience. Therefore, the mind is always the only aspect of self that is ever in need of healing. Heal the mind through forgiveness, and all seeming effects are healed with the healing of the mind. I bring this up because we only waste time stumbling around trying to fix or understand the effects of our misperceptions. These effects show up as the stories that seem to validate and hold our fear in place, making it appear real. We can get stuck in the effects of our thinking, rather than addressing the cause. Jesus tells us that this is neither good nor bad, just a tragic waste of time. It is also not a call for judgment of ourselves or anyone else. We just return to the path of forgiveness. Why else would the *choose once again* option be included in The Plan of Atonement? It was put there because God, in His Infinite Wisdom, knew we would need it on our path to awakening to Heaven. Jesus also reminds me often that the root cause of all of our perceived misery boils down to our misidentification of Self. However, Jesus also assures us that as we forgive (let go of) everything we are *not*, who we truly are naturally will rise up and into our awareness. I find it so comforting to remember that Christ is in all of us. Christ is ever-present and eternal , holding us all in Unity with God.

What I've found helpful is to just say, I'm not that, to anything that does not reflect the purity, innocence, peace, and perfection of God. Just forgive it. Remember that forgiveness is not a doing on our part. It is the willingness to have it done *for* us. As Jesus teaches us, "Forgiveness, on the other hand, is still, and quietly does nothing. It offends no aspect of Reality, nor seeks to twist it to appearances it likes. It merely looks, and waits, and judges not." Whatever shows up and seems to distress us, we simply let it be, let it flow, and let it pass out of our mind. Any appearance not of God and truth will pass through and disappear, but only *if* we do not latch onto it and make it seem real in our experience. We just remind ourselves, I'm not that. We wave goodbye as it passes out of our awareness. All the while we stay fixed, here and Now, in the loving arms and Mind of God. Love has returned to Love and feels safe and secure in Its Embrace. There is so much more to share on our path back to Heaven and Love's awareness. There is so much more to come. From the moment of our decision to choose Love over fear, which aligns our mind with Spirit and activates its power to serve us, comes healing. This brings back our memory of not only who we are but who our brothers and sisters are and most importantly Who/What God Is. We discover this human adventure is a shared one. No longer is this sojourn in life a separate and lonely path, me transforms into we. We walk together, we Love together and extend God's Love out onto the world we perceive before us. We seek no longer to solve or fix or even try to figure out what shows up before us. We *trust* the Spirit of God within us, our Holy Spirit, to take control of us. *Let all things be exactly as they are.* We do not interfere with God's loving remedy. Just as we do not touch a wound and expect it to stay clean and heal. We do not engage a seeming problem after we have given it to God to heal *for* us. At the level of mind, we simply let it be, let it flow, and let it go. This means think no more about it. It was but a misperception of the mind. To engage it is to engage nothingness. It is merely appearing to be something it is not. How do we access this realm of no thought? Very often, right after I have made the choice to activate the Spirit of God within me to handle whatever perceived problem is showing up before me. I leave the battleground that is the path to hell and simply do this. I'm still, and lay aside all thoughts of what I am and what God is, all concepts I have learned about the world, all images I hold about myself. I empty my mind of everything it thinks is either true or false, good or bad, of every thought it judges worthy, and all the ideas of which it is ashamed. *I hold onto nothing.* I do not bring one thought the past has taught, nor one belief I ever learned before from anything. I forget this world, forget this Course, and come with wholly empty hands unto my God.

I often visualize sitting at the feet of Jesus, my head laying in his lap, and he's comforting me, patting me on the head as a parent may do with its child. We are *all* the Children of God, and His will is *always* to Love and Comfort His creations. *His Will is for our perfect happiness.* We need only to *accept* His gift of the Atonement and own it as our own. We need only to always make the choice for Love, truth, and trust in it with every fiber of our being. If we check in right here and right Now in the mind of the one reading this essay, ask only," Am I at Peace?" This will tell you *everything* you need to know. Finally, always remember that. This Course is a beginning, not an end. Your Friend goes with you, you are not alone. No one who calls on Him can call in vain. Whatever troubles you, make the conscious choice to join in unity with creation and leave behind the habitual mentality of separation. In that instant, the soul begins to awaken from Its slumber. It begins to become aware of Itself. Be certain that He has the answer, and will gladly give it to you, if you simply turn to Him and ask it of Him. He will not withhold all answers that you need for anything that seems to trouble you. He knows the way to solve all problems, and resolve all doubts. His certainty is yours. You need but ask it of Him, and it will be given you.

## Part 3: When the path to hell transforms into the path to Heaven.

Within that Holy Instant of choice, we direct the mind to walk out of its separated state of isolation and rejoin our brothers/sisters in the Mind of God. In truth, we have never left. *The only thing that actually left was our awareness of being there.* We simply forgot that our wholeness and completion always dwell with us in Unity with our Creator and all creation. Within this Holy Instant (the here and Now of us), the shift in perception occurs. But it can only come to my awareness by and through my decision to choose it. The Miracle happens in our decision to rejoin our Wholeness in God, with our brothers and sisters in Christ. Our perception shifts back into alignment and the mind returns to sanity and peace. This is why Jesus teaches us that Miracles are shared between brothers. The ever-present Love that we *are* inspires our choice to join, inspires our desire to *decide once again* and rejoin our family in God, and in truth. This Love that inspires Miracles is the same Love that activates and expresses Miracles. You are not only a Miracle Worker, you *are* the Miracle because you *are* Love. Once again, we see the effects of choosing Love over fear and choosing Unity over separation. We remember that we are Spirit, seeming to be having a human experience, but Now that experience is one of Love and Peace instead of worry and regret.

This begs the question, Who is the One that is making this choice? Who is the One that is directing the mind to decide Love instead of fear? It is the One that is Now aware that there is a choice to be made. It is the Pure Awareness of Being. It is the One that is aware of being aware of the words of this essay and reading them *Now*. The One that is aware of everything that seems to appear before it. The Pure and Perfect Awareness of Being, with nothing added to obscure or defile its Perfect State of Peace. In short, it is the Soul awakening from its slumber and beginning to remember Itself. It is the One that at first just recognizes and notices I exist, that there is an experience of existence within this awareness. It notices that It is the One who is aware of being aware. When and if, It looks at Its Nature, all that it is aware of is a still, quiet, and peaceful presence. At that moment all it recognizes is that it is aware that It exists, and Its existence is aware of only Pure and Perfect Peace. Yes, Soul is awakening to the awareness of Self. It is just beginning to remember. If, and this is a big if, it goes deeper within, Its awareness seems to expand, and it recognizes that it is a part of something that is far more vast. As yet, it is not aware of what this vastness is, aware that there is more to become aware of in its experience of being aware. For Now, all that It is certain of is that It exists as the Awareness of Perfect Peace, and stillness of Being. Little does It realize that It has stumbled upon Its Home in Love and Its Reality as Love. However, if at any instant It chooses to look without instead of continuing on Its journey within Its own Nature, it begins to become aware of other seeming appearances. They seem to be outside the pure and peaceful sanctity of Its Beingness. It Now becomes aware of a something that appears separate from Itself. At that instant, when Its focus is pointed without and away from its within, Its awareness seems to expand again but brings a completely different experience. These appearances seem to disturb its Pure and Perfect awareness of existence. It becomes aware of darkness being laid upon the Light of Its Being. This Being of Pure awareness becomes confused and frightened by Its new awareness of a something other than Pure and Perfect Peace. For the first time, this Being of Pure and Perfect Peace asks, What Am I? Who Am I? Am I the within, or the without? Its journey of Awakening and Remembering truth has begun. In that instant, Its awareness becomes so limited, and It seems blocked by a new awareness. It is awareness of a darkness It does not understand. Little does It know of Its Divine Power, the Power of Love that Is Its truth. Little does it know that there is *nothing* that is not a part of Its Wholeness and Oneness in God. It is not even aware that such a something as God exists. All that it is aware of is that it is frightened and alone, *yet*, it feels an inner urge to call for Help. Little does it know that Its call for Help was heard and answered. Little does it know that in that very instant, the Holy Instant, It made the choice for the opposite of the darkness that It was experiencing. It made the choice for Love. And in that Holy Instant, the awareness of a Light Within grew brighter and stronger and made a path back to Heaven, where only the awareness of Pure and Perfect Peace resided. The call for Love was made, and the Father always responds to every call of His Son with the Self-Same Love contained within the call. The Son recognized the Love within as His Father. Love recognized Love and remembered Itself. The choice was made to join in Unity as One. The choice was made to return to Love. Now, the awareness of the Perfect State of Oneness has awakened and exists within the Sonship with Its Creator. It is/will be/has been accomplished. Time rolls up into eternity, here and Now. Within the Holy Instant, miracles occur, and the mind shifts back into alignment with truth and Reality. For a Holy Instant, time/space, the body, and the ego are forgotten long enough that one can catch glimpses of Reality, and they become points of reference for our access. These access points are never forgotten because they are Real. They are like building blocks that create a mental bridge that leads us back to the path of Heaven and to the Peace of God. Your Real and Present Memory is being restored to your awareness. It was never lost, only forgotten. *Always keep in mind that Real Memory is of a present state of awareness, and has nothing to do with an imagined past.*

Every occasion we choose to join in a Holy Instant in the present moment, our remembrance and awareness of Reality and of our True Self is strengthened. We begin by bringing our awareness to the present moment. We fix our focus and attention right here and right Now. It may seem strange in the beginning, but soon we discover all the spiritual goodies associated with truth are found and realized here and Now; not the least of which is our peace of mind. Soon being present becomes a treasured habit. Once this habit is formed and stabilized, it is a place in which we desire to visit and stay within as much as possible. Every instant then becomes a Holy Instant in which we join and share Love and Peace with all of our brothers/sisters because they are there with us in the Mind of God. The Holy Instant is the Instant God is remembered. The ego thought system, time, space, the body, and everything we have come to believe in as real, fades away in this present state of Being. It is in our joining and sharing of what Is Real (here and Now) that Real

Memory is restored and everything unreal disappears. Soon we learn to join with our brothers in this sacred space for healing and in sharing the Love of God. Here and Now is a state of present consciousness that serves two primary functions. One function is that of experience, and the other function is choice. You could say consciousness is a state of being where we experience the effects of our choices. Consciousness of itself has no other powers or purpose. It responds based on the choices made through either the ego thought system or through the guidance of our Holy Spirit. Once a conscious choice is made, a conscious experience is had that is reflective of our choice.

Never forget God's safety net built into the plan of Atonement. We can always *choose once again*. Undo what never was and continue on the path to Heaven. *Our end is really our beginning.* When the choice for the ego thought system is made, we can count on all of our experiences to be fear-based. Because it is a dualistic thought system, our experiences may show up a good/bad, right/wrong, hot/cold, and up/down. However, what will be lacking *always* are certainty, clarity, and a peaceful state of mind. Even an experience that feels exhilarating and exciting can also be terrifying. Because duality is made up of only opposites, certainty is never possible. The mind bounces back and forth from one to the other, or often becomes stuck in the middle. Being a thought system based on confusion, it can never provide certainty. It is a thought system that thrives on conflict, confusion, and indecision. Clarity of mind is never an attribute. Obviously, without clarity or certainty, the idea of peace of mind must also be absent. How can one possibly compare the ego thought system to what is discovered within the Holy Instant of here and Now? How does one describe a new primary color that has never been seen before? When one joins with another for the singular purpose of healing, something miraculous happens. One has to pay close attention to catch a glimpse of what is *not* present. There is no little self anymore. Something happens when two join in union with God. All sense of self disappears. One's awareness of anything outside that united holy moment vanishes. Now is all there is, and place becomes no more. Information comes from a new Source, a Source not of the thinking mind but outside of it. It is so huge and expansive, one can get lost in just the thought of it. What appears in the mind is not of our making, it just arrives without any effort, and you have a *knowingness* and a certainty that it is true and real. Here and Now, this Holy Instant, is the place of miracles. It is where forgiveness occurs and healing appears. It is where we commune with

God in Christ and there is no sense of any gap or separation existing. It is whole, it is peaceful, still, and wonderful. It is Love. One wants to abide there forever, the path to sanity and happiness. The Holy Spirit is nothing more than your own right Mind. The Holy Spirit is not separate from my own Divine Mind, I share with God. I have access to it whenever I choose it. Its healing power can only be released by my decision to join it.

When I think of right-mindedness, I think of clear thinking and clear perception or vision where everything makes sense again and its nature becomes obvious as if a light bulb has been turned on in the mind. I experience it as a link, not only a communication link but a link to a Source of high energy, healing energy that I can ride along with for as long as I stay focused and fixed on its attributes and not be distracted and pulled back into an ego perception or mentality. It is like riding the God wave of Divine Energy, which should be our natural manner of existence. This is what is defined as the Happy Dream. A realm where, although still dreaming, we experience the dream as a reflection of God's Love and its truth. To stay in the Happy Dream, I need to stay fixed and focused on it by aligning the mind with its attributes. These attributes are also the attributes of God and truth. I'm not always successful, but when I am able to maintain my focus and attention on truth, the following reminders have proven helpful to me and I hope you find them helpful as well. Affirming that I am One with this Source of Divine Energy that is God. I am not separate, nor have I ever been separate from my Source. And this magnificent Divine Energy of God provides for everything I could ever need. It is what the birds and flowers naturally accept and never question. Watching my thoughts and feelings, they are my barometer for knowing if I am obstructing my access to my Divine Source. They tell me if I am aligned with the Mind of God or in conflict with it. I practice forgiveness whenever the slightest hint of discomfort or disharmony shows up in my mind through either thoughts or feelings. When in doubt, forgive. Forgiveness heals whatever requires healing and returns my mind to peace. Expressing gratitude to God for who and what I Am. Gratitude acknowledges what I have, and to have it is to know I Am it. Sharing the gifts of the Kingdom. Our Divine Source of everything is a continuous flow of creation. It is always sharing itself and in this way ensures the process of creation continues. Any hoarding or attachments to what has been given us only impedes its flow to and through us. Extending what I am to be what I am. This is similar to sharing in that to have Peace, I extend Peace. To know Love, I extend Love. God created us through the extension of

His Love for us and to know we are a creation vehicle for God, we practice it in our daily life. Allowing and not resisting what shows up in our lives. Resisting not evil is wise advice. For everything that shows up in our daily experience, we either Love it or heal it, but we never resist it. To resist is to give that which is not real a false Reality. It is what ACIM calls, making it real. That is an obstruction to everything that Is real. Listening and following the guidance of the Holy Spirit. I do this through meditation and prayer. Prayer to me is communion with God. I sit in silence and listen for thoughts that show up in my mind that are not of my making. While meditating or communing with the Father, I feel our Oneness and shared Love for all creation. Grab hold of your Divine Source and live there. Be alert to anything that suggests we are being drawn away from it by the ego. Pay the ego no mind, except for healing the idea that it is real and can affect our experience of God's Love as His perfect Child. Always remember, the ego is not a real thought and actually does not exist. When we are in our right mind, we realize this and pay it no mind.

Just behind all the imagined obstructions we have made to limit and block our awareness of the truth, truth stands eternal and shines Its Light. This Light of truth is forever pristine, ever-present, and unaffected by our ignorance of it and Its God-given powers, which belong to us as creations and extensions of God. As such, we can Truly say, We *are* the Light of the World. In truth, there are no blocks or obstructions that can dim our eternal Light. They are only the "seems to bees" of this life experience. "Seems to bees" are delusions and distortions of the mind and have no basis in Reality. They are like cloud vapors that try to block out the sun. Yet the light of the sun is never diminished by the clouds. Our imaginary obstructions show up as thoughts, perceptions, physical sights and sensations, and our beliefs about them. We give them so much meaning, they can captivate us and divert our focus and attention away from the ever-present Light of our Being. They distort Reality until it becomes unrecognizable and even forgotten. Yet, be never deceived for an instant, my friends. The brilliant Light of our Self continues to shine out from us into all creation. The eyes of God see through the eyes of His creations and beholds creation as He Created it. God expresses and experiences Himself through His Son. God is in everything I see because God is in my mind. Always remember that our imagined obstructions that seem to hide our Light have no power, other than the power we give them. We feed and nourish them when we focus our attention on them instead of on God, thereby affording them a false Reality. They are illusions. They do not exist except within the ego thought system, and that is an illusion as well. How can nothing have any power? As Jesus reminds us, "By giving power to nothing, he throws away the joyous opportunity to learn that nothing has no power."

What is the remedy for the mess we made up? What is there to do about nothing appearing as something? We have been conditioned since birth to believe we must do something, to fix things and all kinds of "doingness". The idea of doing nothing and accepting what is for the most part are alien concepts. They seem so counter-intuitive, and go against our human nature. Yet, where illusions are concerned, to do nothing is exactly what is called for. Forgiveness, on the other hand, is still, and quietly does nothing. It offends no aspect of Reality, nor seeks to twist it to appearances it likes. It merely looks, and waits, and judges not. Over the years, I have discovered that there is but one solution to any and all perceived problems, and that is returning the mind to God. As we bring all of our focus and attention to this present moment, we are abandoning the imagined thought system of ego and choosing God instead. We bring whatever seems unlike Love to Love. There, all ego thoughts, feelings, and sensations naturally dissolve and disappear. And in this present moment, as we give them over to our Holy Spirit, they are starved by our lack of focus and attention on them. No longer are we giving power to nothing. Rather, we are reclaiming our Power as the Son of God. There is but One Power, Emmanuel, which means God with Us.

In returning the mind to God, we literally swim within an ocean of Love. It is the atmosphere of our existence. How could anything exist outside All? In Unity and Wholeness, we were created and in Unity and Wholeness, we eternally remain. We affirm God Is and anything, unlike Love, disappears into the nothingness from which it came. We say God Is and cease to speak. Nothing else needs to be said because within God Is, everything is accomplished. You are the One you are searching for. Truth is only found within, and even then I ask what is the truth of this? Whatever this may be at any moment. All perceptions are distorted, even those of great spiritual teachers. Only within can truth be recognized, remembered, and experienced; all else is interpretation. We all carry the truth within our own holy minds. As Jesus reminds us in ACIM, "Delay does not matter in eternity, but it is tragic in time."

Everything is a pointer to God and truth. Even "A Course In Miracles" is but a pointer to truth. I have found it to be a very effective one. Either through gratitude or desperation, we all find our way Home. Let us not spend all of our time trying to understand the words of ACIM but rather seek the inner peace it offers and truth is effortlessly revealed from that point of peace. The Peace of God is always right here and right Now as your Holy and Divine Self. It is an accomplished fact. Yet, it is always our choice to take a long way home or a more direct route. Many times we are like the puppy dog chasing after its own tail, believing it is separate from Itself. Eventually, the puppy catches its tail and truth bites him in the ass, surprise. Jesus tells us that awakening need not be painful, but it usually is. Putting false gods before our own, I Am, is merely an ego tactic to delay the inevitable. Do you really believe the finite mind is capable of understanding Infinite truth? You, right here and right Now, *are* the Holy Son of God. *Be that.* God's Presence and God's Voice go with us wherever we go. They are the Reality of Self. His Voice and His Love define me. It is not the other way around. They are the Truest truth to me. They are the gifts I share with everyone and everything I see. It is the Loving exchange and sharing of Love with Love, that giving and receiving merge into One complete, whole, and seamless experience. It is there that I discover my Holy Relationship with All of God's creation. Practice makes progress. Yet, that which is Real and True is already accomplished. We are an accomplished fact of God. Might as well enjoy all the Gifts of the Kingdom. Now. Always remember our ego wants us to be either regretting our past or, best yet, worrying about the future. When we live in the moment, what can hurt us? Nothing. Once again, The Course refers to this as living in The Holy Instant.

CHAPTER 39

# The African Mother

LET'S SAY YOU ARE an African mother living in the jungle in the year 1694. You have been with your husband for 17 years and have four children. Life is challenging, but you work hard and find joy in the simple moments. Though the heat is relentless and raising a family is demanding, you laugh more often than you cry. Your life is good. One day, a group of missionaries arrives in your village. They seem kind, offering food and warm smiles. They begin speaking of a man named Jesus, who lived thousands of years ago. They tell you that he walked on water, healed the blind and deaf, made the paralyzed walk, and even raised the dead. They explain that he was crucified but rose again three days later. Then, they deliver the news that he died for your sins, and unless you believe in him, you will suffer in eternal hell. Confused, you ask, "What is sin?" They explain. "What is hell?" They tell you. That night, you lie awake, contemplating these strange new ideas. They seem absurd, who created such stories? You have lived a hard but fulfilling life, surrounded by love and friendship. You have made mistakes, but until now, you never considered them sins. You had always believed your parents created you, yet now you are told that God did, and that He is furious with you. This unseen God, they say, is prepared to send you into unending torment. Yet, they claim there is hope. If you simply believe in Jesus, who endured suffering and death for sins you never knew existed, you will be saved. You struggle with the thought. A God who demands sacrifice and suffering does not resonate with the peace you have always felt within. The guilt you never knew begins to weigh on you, and you do not welcome the feeling. Though the missionaries are kind-hearted, you trust your own wisdom. You have never lied and always told the truth. So when the minister asks if you believe in Jesus, you answer honestly: "I would rather not. I was doing better before I learned of these things." They leave.

For years, resentment lingers. The missionaries disrupted the peace of your mind. Yet, over time, you begin speaking to their God, addressing Him in prayer. You understand forgiveness, you have practiced it countless times with your husband and children. One day, you tell God you have forgiven the missionaries, and an inexplicable joy and peace briefly envelop you. Over the next decade, your connection with God deepens. He becomes your closest companion, though your feelings about sin and Jesus' death remain unchanged. Years pass, and at the age of 94, you peacefully slip into sleep, never to awaken in this world again. Where are you now? The atheist says, "In the dirt." The born-again Christian says, "eternal hell." Yet there is a third answer, one that is magnificent, luminous, and divine, "You are enjoying the perfection and Love of Heaven, forever."

CHAPTER 40

# We're Dreaming In Heaven

OUR MINDS ARE EXTRAORDINARILY powerful, being an extension of God's Mind. Falsely perceiving that we had eternally lost perfect communication with Source, we entered our first dream, an illusory universe set within time. In this nightmare of duality, Oneness was replaced by twoness, and the false concept of perpetual conflict became the accepted norm. The same Holy Spirit Who corrected the original Christ is now observing our dream, guiding the process of healing. We dream of reincarnation, understanding that its purpose is awakening, not a permanent exit from time through death, but rather the attainment of perfection in forgiveness. This highlights the supreme importance of exoneration. When a time script is completed, we are shown the lessons learned, never needing to be repeated, because their teachings were understood. As we listen to the Voice for God, we co-author the next time script with the understanding that there will be no conscious memory of previous scripts. Yet, the unconscious retains all experiences with clarity, purified by the Holy Spirit. Both "A Course in Miracles" and "The Disappearance of the Universe" assert that I am the only one here, and everyone I have encountered since birth is merely a dream figure. Initially, this concept was difficult to accept, so I explored it through my own experiences, hoping that writing would once again serve as my teacher.

Why dream of a loving mother and father? A deep, unconscious false belief suggested I had forsaken and lost the ultimate Love of God. The unconditional Love of my parents offered profound peace, which the Holy Spirit used to dissolve the false belief. Why dream of childhood joys, playing in the sprinkler, catching lightning bugs, hiking, hide-and-seek, the excitement of Christmas Eve and Halloween, the thrill of the last day of school, and the comforting smell of a classroom upon returning? As a child, I lived entirely in the moment, unburdened by past mistakes or future concerns. These dreams reinforced the wonder and joy of presence and strengthened my desire to understand eternity , where wonder and joy are eternally experienced. Why dream of being a frightened little boy in kindergarten? This proved that confidence grows through new experiences and connections beyond a protective environment. Why dream of Count Dracula, who could enter my room on a moonbeam? This was my first encounter with fear. Crawling between my sleeping parents revealed the perfect safety of Love. Why dream of a childhood bully tormenting me for weeks? This experience taught me the illusion of weakness. After listening to my mother's guidance and standing up to him, I uncovered an inner strength, a previously unknown strength that ended his bullying forever. Why dream of my first Love, my high school sweetheart? She introduced the joy of sharing life with another, the anticipation of seeing her again, the thrill of discovery, the happiness found in simple companionship. Why dream of attending college? To unlock hidden intelligence and experience the satisfaction of striving and achieving. Why dream of insanity, wars, drugs, homelessness, poverty, corruption, crime, abuse, anger, lies, greed, and hate? Recognizing the world's insanity proved my growing sanity and discernment of what is unwanted. Why dream of betrayal, trusted friends who lied and stole? This taught the beauty of forgiveness and the peace it brings. Why dream of miraculous survival, being crushed by a 30-ton crane? This revealed the truth of miracles. Why dream of LSD-fueled weekends at age 27? I learned of beauty, wonder, joy, and awe beyond the five senses. But why dream of the nightmare that followed, a pure PCP overdose, plunging me into 30 hours of unimaginable horror? It was the most dreadful experience of my life, a hallucination of screaming babies on fire, serpents with rat heads, bat-like female creatures, alternating flashes of searing light and absolute darkness. This terror began at 6:00 p.m. on a Friday. After hours of torment, I looked at the clock, 6:01 p.m. Only one minute had passed. I clung to a small white light at the very top of my consciousness, believing if I stopped breathing, I would remain in that hell forever. Emerging from catatonia on Sunday morning, I immediately destroyed the drug. That nightmare taught me the ego's ruthless cruelty and the Holy Spirit's gentle salvation via the purity of light. Why dream of losing my beautiful, loving wife of 20 years, who suddenly died at 43? To understand the depth of Love. We do not fully grasp what we have until we perceive its absence. Why dream of celebrities, musicians, and athletes? At first, envy clouded my perception. But as my spiritual studies progressed, I found genuine happiness for them. Their success was born from discipline and striving for perfection. Most share their talents with the world as an extension of their gifts. Why dream of you reading this? To experience the joy of sharing truth through extension, and to realize that I am my own best teacher. Simply knowing this is a miracle.

CHAPTER 41

## The Call Of The Goddess

WHEN THE GODDESS CALLS you Home, you may not immediately recognize Her Voice. Often, those summoned to remember Her touch have become numb to Her sacred presence. Her call does not arrive with a warning, it comes as chaos, dissolution, breaking apart, breaking open, breaking down. It strips away illusions, clearing the energy bodies and opening the channels of spiritual awareness. When you are meant to follow the Voice of the Goddess, life may suddenly seem incomprehensible. This is because a Divinely guided path awaits, one beyond what you once believed possible. The daughters and sons of the Great Goddess have spent lifetimes in spiritual exile, shutting down their gifts, hardening their emotional sensitivity, dismissing their intuition, and blending in with the sleeping masses. Many entered this lifetime believing they would lead ordinary, structured lives, disconnected from the rhythm of their souls.

When the Call of the Goddess comes, profound change follows. External conditions shift, sometimes as an unexpected cosmic force, sometimes as a series of unfolding events that make continuing as before impossible. It may be the arrival or departure of a person, financial dissolution, illness, emotional upheaval, or any combination of intense transformations that stir the soul, preparing it to return Home. The Goddess works in mysterious ways. She knows who you are, who you were, and who you are meant to become. She understands that your life must receive an electric shock to pull you from the ego into the Divine. She knows that breakdowns, chaos, and uncertainty bring fear. but they are necessary to awaken you, to make you realize that what you once accepted is no longer enough. She calls forth your ancient wisdom, spiritual energy, and Divine purpose.

Answering the Call of the Goddess often means watching everything you thought was important collapse. Your conditioned beliefs may be challenged. Yet, as this rebirth begins, circles of supportive souls will be sent to you, those who have known you before, from times of devotion to the Goddess. Though fear may arise, you will also witness the Divine working through your life, guiding you. The Call of the Goddess is growing stronger, touching those ready to awaken. If you are reading these words, She is reaching for you. She offers a forgotten breath, a stirring soul melody, the rhythm of Her songs, and the pulse of Her Heart. She speaks through your experiences, through a person, a book, a workshop, or a longing for deeper meaning. Your life may already be dissolving its old form, preparing to be rebuilt in Her image. However She appears, it is Her work, Her hand, Her guidance leading you toward a life infused with soul and purpose. Your destiny is unfolding each day. Listen to your inner urges and impulses, they are the whispers of the Great Goddess. It is all your soul has ever wanted, calling you Home.

## CHAPTER 42

# Pray

WHAT IS SIMPLER THAN salvation? How hard is it to recognize what has true value? Experience is essential, for without the direct experience of Reality, the mind can only choose between what is temporary and what is also temporary. Look around, everything seen through the body's eyes is fleeting. All things change, and one by one, they return to dust, as countless things have before them. Yet within you, beyond the illusions of the world, waits an experience so profound that it will render all worldly values meaningless. When you desire only Love, you will have it, for Love is Reality Itself. But this Love is not the Love of the world. It is not the Love of bodies, possessions, power, or status. It is the Love of Self, unconditional and limitless, extending to all living things, being what all things truly are. Look with open eyes and an open mind, what do you see that will last forever? All is within you. Pray.

CHAPTER 43

# Every Course Student Should Read

*by Kenneth Wapnick*

THE EGO CONTINUALLY ATTEMPTS to distort our Course practice, turning it into something that reinforces guilt rather than removing it. The Miracle is not about forcing oneself to begrudgingly choose the Holy Spirit over the ego. Rather, choosing the Holy Spirit will become automatic when the Miracle is embraced. The Miracle is the act of observing oneself choosing the ego over the Holy Spirit and forgiving that choice. It acknowledges that if I am unhappy, anxious, hurt, or suffering, I have made the decision to feel this way. I want to feel this way. I could choose peace instead, but I am not ready to. And then, crucially, I forgive myself. Looking without judgment, looking alongside the Holy Spirit at my choice for the ego, is what undoes its hold. I refuse to turn away as the ego urges me to. Instead, I remain with Jesus in my mind, allowing no shame to push me away. Choosing the Holy Spirit is nothing more than observing my attachment to the ego without guilt. It is not a battle against the ego, nor a forced rejection. It is simply forgiving my choice as misguided but not sinful. Looking with the Holy Spirit means holding Her Love and Peace in my awareness while observing my self-imposed suffering, without making it into a sin. The Miracle is merely recognizing that I am doing this unto myself and forgiving myself even as I do it. But I must continue looking at Jesus, never turning away. Nothing I think, do, or feel should separate me from Love in my mind. The practice is about bringing everything to Love through non-judgment of myself.

The Miracle does not require us to cease choosing the ego. Rather, it requires that we see we are choosing the ego. This is where many students of the Course go astray, believing that their goal is to decide for the Holy Spirit when, in reality, they are not yet ready. The true goal is to embrace the Miracle, to fully understand what we are choosing and to forgive ourselves for continually choosing specialness. By doing this, we invite Jesus to look at the ego alongside us. That is the Miracle: returning to the mind and, with Jesus or the Holy Spirit beside us, recognizing that we are choosing separation, whether or not we are ready to relinquish it. At the very least, awareness of this truth means we can no longer place blame elsewhere, not on the environment, not on those who have harmed us, not on genetics or karma. If I am upset now, it is because I choose to be upset now. I do not want God's Peace, I want my specialness. I want my own experience of ego. But at least I now understand my own decision. That is the purpose of the Course. Once I reach this realization, it is only a matter of time before I recognize that choosing the ego no longer serves me. And naturally, the shift happens. This takes immense practice, as the urge to blame others runs deep. The resistance to accepting full responsibility is strong, and if dedication feels weak, I may not yet be ready. But Jesus reminds us, "Do not fight yourself." We must not pretend to be ready when we are not yet prepared. True spiritual advancement means being able to say: "I know what I am doing, and I am not yet ready to stop. I know I want my specialness. I want to be different. I want to blame others. I want what I want, when I want it. And that is okay." Fighting the ego only reinforces the belief that the ego is real. This reflects the biblical teaching "resist not evil". To resist something is to acknowledge its existence and power. If I resist the ego, I make it real. The Course does not teach us to battle the ego, nor to silence it, nor to overpower it. It simply says: "Look at your ego and smile at it, because it is nothing." Fighting the ego makes it real.

So when I forget my daily practice, when I fail to apply its simple truths, I must not be surprised, angry, or guilty. Instead, I simply acknowledge: "Ah, this is my ego in action. I am still afraid of the Love and Peace of God." This honesty propels me forward, undoing a thousand years of resistance. By stepping back and observing my ego without judgment, without resistance, without a need to change it, I undo the original mistake, the moment when the Son of God took the "tiny mad idea" seriously instead of laughing at it. Jesus reminds us: "It is a joke to think that time can circumvent eternity. It is a joke to believe that a tiny mad idea can interfere with the Infinite." The discipline of the Course is learning to look at the ego and not take it seriously. If resistance is strong and dedication weak, I must simply acknowledge: "I am still afraid of the Love of God, but that is all right." These words hold the greatest importance because they dissolve judgment. I am not labeling my ego as sinful or wicked. I am simply recognizing: "This is what I am choosing. But it does not alter Jesus' Love for me. It does not change the Holy Spirit's Love for me." This is the path to awakening.

CHAPTER 44

# The Phasing Dimensional Library

**Table of Contents**

Preface
Chapter 1:     L2BA TSF3 01
Chapter 2:     123 Blast Off
Chapter 3:     The Essay Flow

Chapter 4:     My Horrifying & Catatonic Drug Experience
Chapter 5:     Drug Misinformation

### Preface

This fictional story is drawn from a real experience in 1978. A friend offered the chance to buy pure PCP directly from its chemist. Having taken LSD hundreds of times, hallucinogens were familiar. Today, medical research is showing remarkable results with LSD, DMT, Peyote, and Psilocybin Mushrooms in treating schizophrenia, manic-depressive disorder, bipolar disorder, borderline personality disorder, and post-traumatic stress disorder. The approach, known as microdosing, has yielded promising clinical outcomes. Yet, after fifteen years without psychedelics, there is no longer a desire or need. PCP, often cut with embalming fluid, remains one of the most horrifying substances known. A doctor once remarked that it was a miracle not to be institutionalized after ingesting such a pure form in high quantities. He had patients still in catatonic states and understood firsthand the severity of the drug's effects. Wentworth undergoes an extreme confrontation with his deranged ego, an assault experienced, in varying forms, by all. But with deep gratitude, refuge is found in the powerful Voice for God, the Holy Spirit, dwelling in the right side of the mind.

## Chapter 1: L2BA TSF3 O1

Bob Hall hates his name, say it out loud, and you'll understand why, sounds *really* stupid. He's changing his name to Wentworth Wellington Hall, *this* will instill awe and respect in others. So, from Now on, he's referring to himself as Wentworth. He'll buy a monocle next week on Tuesday at exactly 3:17pm because of the critical time importance, he'll be wearing his double-breasted blue color blazer with yellow long johns and purple penny loafers. He *knows* this will cause the ladies to faint and strong men to whimper like beaten turtles.

Wentworth was starting to feel unusually strange in his Heart, mind, spirit, and soul because the extremely powerful psychedelics were kicking in. He wasn't quite certain if taking 100 hits of Grateful Dead LSD, a huge ball of Magic Psilocybin Mushrooms and Very Pure DMT at the same time was the grandest idea he'd ever had. He'll find out sooner rather than later. Massive earthquakes started shaking the house, yard, and street. The sky turned purple, and the pouring rain was green. He just saw a ten-foot tall orange lady with a tail and mustache riding a skateboard. Superman was powerless and running from a kryptonite moose with white wings. Suddenly his living room phased, shifted and exploded into absolute total complete unending darkness. He heard what he thought was him saying, "Bob Hall, you have entered into the state of complete nothingness, and you will vanish from your own awareness. Forever. Oh no, Bob Hall, you've finally overdosed on too many drugs and are having a brain aneurysm that is killing you. Wait a minute, I'm Wentworth and not stupid Bob Hall, he can die if that's what he wants. I need a beer, but it's so damn dark I can't figure out where the refrigerator is." The Beatles are singing that they want to hold his hand. "This sounds like a glorious idea if they're singing from my kitchen." They stopped playing, and Pink Floyd is saying he's comfortably numb. "Damn right, because I'm Wentworth, and enjoying the grandest of names." A distant ship on the horizon and his hands that felt like two balloons are telling him his beer is in the washing machine covered in red ice. "That's nice if there are no mice covered in pizza." He's *got* to find his beer to stop this stupid brain aneurysm from killing Bob Hall, after all, he couldn't help it for being so dumb. "Why is it so damn dark?" Instantly, he heard, "Because you don't exist." Kansas is telling him he's dust in the wind. "Fine, settle my dust on the washing machine, so I can drink 9 or 10 beers to save that idiot Bob Hall. Wait a moment, how can dust drink?"

There's a gigantic expansion of brilliant pure light, and he's standing naked in a massive library holding his cell phone. "Oh *great*, Now I've got to find some clothes *and* my washing machine while figuring out how to leave a library." For a most important and critical reason, Wentworth remembered that crazy Bob Hall had never set up his phone's voicemail. After dialing in, he recorded his brilliant message, "If you're calling for Bob, I'm now Wentworth. I'm over there and not here, so when I return here from there I'll leave again if it's raining. I left there some time ago and became lost getting here, so I returned there to remember here. I think. It's sunny, and I'm going bowling, so I won't get skin cancer. If you're there when I find the route from my there to you here, I'll call if I remember to turn on the oven and flush the toilet 3 times. Your stupid call is extremely unimportant to me, so I'll return the call as quickly as possible when I go there from here. Maybe. hello for now." Someone, somewhere, said it's time to read a book. "What? I'll read a book titled "How To Stop A Brain Aneurysm From Killing A Naked Idiot In A Library Looking For His Beer In A Washing Machine. Help me mom! Crap! She told my dead aunt, who's now crawling up my leg with a knife in her teeth." A different someone explained that his beer was really in the bedroom dresser and was getting warm. "This *cannot* be happening, warm beer makes me vomit, looks like Bob Hall is going to die. Oh well, no big deal, he doesn't have any friends anyway because he's stupid. Are all these books laughing at me? Why is the floor on the ceiling? What is the purpose of air? Do fish drown? The magazines are crying? Are all birds really robots spying on me? Do animals talk in English amongst themselves? Is the moon really an alien satellite? Can I walk in the sun? All the known universe is on the head of a pin in another dimension? Why do I have so many questions and receive absolutely no answers? How can my body be experiencing all this when it's nothing but dust? Is God real?" I hear a powerful "YES" in my Heart's mind and have received a certain and truthful answer. Finally!

BAA AAM! "Or was this a small knock? Why are they tearing down the library?" Now he's looking at Gladimere, the friend who put the idea in his head that Bob Hall was an idiotic name. His one buddy says, "Jesus H. Christ, your one eye open and one closed make you look like an insane maniac." "Yes? However, my middle name isn't H for Herbert and my last name is not Christ, my name is Jesus of Nazareth. Gladimere, why is Robert thinking he is standing naked in his living room with a warm beer and saying something about a library, although he's dust in the wind looking for a book he must read?" "I have no idea, he must be going through another of his idiotic and insane tripping experiences." Wentworth looked at Jesus, who suddenly became a composite of Elvis and John Lennon, and asked, "Who did you say my name is?" "Robert" "Way cool, I like that better than Wentworth, can you please help me find my beer in my dresser before it gets any warmer? And I really don't enjoy being dust. How will I be able to drink my beer to save Bob Hall?" Jesus who is now Elton John exclaims," Tiny dancer, I don't know if the yellow brick road leads to your bedroom, but I'll ask God for specific instructions." Gladimere now wonders why Bob who thinks he's naked but isn't is talking to himself and Elton John Jesus about his name being Robert who has turned from dust to a tiny dancer and is on the yellow brick road to find the warm beer in his bedroom dresser so he won't have a brain aneurysm. He's sorry he ever knocked on the door and decides he *must* leave before his brain implodes. "Bye Bob". "My name is *not* Bob, it's Robert, and I look stupid in this ballerina skirt." "Sorry man, I'll visit you if you end up catatonic in a mental institution, I must leave. Now!"

Bob Wentworth who is now Robert is looking at Elton John Jesus and is wondering why he's smiling. "You think this is funny? I enjoyed being a man, not a little girl, but at least I'm no longer dust. I must find my warming beer to save Bob Hall, who thankfully is now Robert Hall." "Yes, this *is* funny, you're really standing in your front yard talking to a tree and embarrassed because your neighbors will see you naked, even though you're not. Sorry, I have some duties in Heaven and must leave also. I'm like Gladimere and you need to stop believing your insane ego mindset." "Ok, sissy Elton John Jesus, leave, but thank you so very much for telling me my name is Robert." "You're welcome, see you again eventually." Robert suddenly realizes he *is* talking to a tree, and it's *very important* to take out the trash before drinking what is now going to be 25 beers to save Bob Hall. His mailbox starts singing "Wait a minute Mr. Postman", the neighbor's dog turns into a Zebra, a passing car transforms into a boat pulling a skier that's a cow, his bowels explode, and the mess somehow vanishes, swat teams are invading numerous homes, the grass grows ten feet and the entire neighborhood starts flooding. "What is going on, I'm back in the library gazing at an attractive librarian ? I must ask her some questions." The librarian is looking at this strange man with a warm, unopened beer in his hand and unbuttoned pants, wearing no shoes with one sock. "Miss, I must say you're very beautiful, but beauty is only skin deep. Comprehend please?" The woman is somewhat perplexed and has no words. "This is real simple, Miss Librarian. I need a book titled, "My Brief Discussion With Elton John Jesus." It's a bestseller. In this magnificent book I'll understand why I first came to this library when I was naked looking for my alcohol in a washing machine, when the warm beer was really in my dresser drawer, and why I was actually talking to a tree about taking out the trash before drinking 25 beers in the refrigerator where they never left to save Bob Hall who is now Robert Hall and no longer Wentworth from dying of a brain aneurysm because the idiot took way to many drugs. DO YOU UNDERSTAND ME?"

The librarian is thinking, "I can't talk to this insane madman who is starting to take off his clothes, I'm calling the police." "Miss, I can see in your eyes the desire to make love, but first things first." Bob, who is Now Robert, stops undressing, opens the warm beer and downs it. "Now this helps because the alcohol is telling me to calm down as Bob, who is really Robert. I understand Bob Hall is not going to die from taking too many hallucinogens and remember reading that nobody has ever died from the drugs, but have passed because they fell out of a tree when they thought they were in bed." The librarian is starting to relax but is startled when this strange man shouts, "Jesus's real name is Jesus of Nazareth not Jesus Christ, and he's now talking with friends in Heaven after telling me I was talking to a tree in my front yard while thinking I was naked. He explained I was clothed but concerned about the flooding neighborhood, a water-skiing cow, a dog Zebra eating cheese, swat teams running backwards, and other strange occurrences. My Brother explained the extremely weird and chaotic thoughts are the manifestation of my egoistic wrong, insane and lying mind. I'm beginning to recognize the absolute truth."

## Chapter 2: 123 BLAST OFF

Robert sat in stillness, the weight of revelation settling over him like a warm embrace. For the first time, he understood something beyond words, beyond reason, something that had always been present but had remained elusive in the tangled corridors of his mind. "I am not a human being," he murmured, the words carrying the gravity of truth. "Jesus was human, but he fully realized he was a Christ Being. And I am beginning to remember that I, too, am a Christ Being. Eventually, all will recall this truth. It is guaranteed by God. We are all One Christ Being, forever One with Source." The librarian, who had moments ago watched a manic stranger unravel before her, now witnessed a transformation unlike anything she had seen before. A profound peace emanated from Robert, and with it, his green eyes shifted into a piercing shade of blue. "I remember now," he continued, his voice steady with newfound certainty. "We are all One in the Magnificent Mind of God, our Father. We are perfect, incapable of sin, and we live forever. Jesus is not to be worshiped but deeply respected. He is our eldest brother. Life outside of Heaven is impossible, we merely believe we are living on earth due to the unfathomable power of our minds. But this is false. We are dreaming in Heaven, and we will awaken from the illusion once we have achieved perfection in forgiveness." Robert's words carried something unshakable, something ancient and intrinsic. The librarian felt something stir within her, a forgotten truth taking shape. "Yes," she whispered. "The seasons, the rainforests, the migration of birds, these things exist in perfect harmony because the love of God permeates everything. The animal kingdom understands the Christ Mind effortlessly. They do not question; they simply exist in truth. But humanity, gifted with free will, forgot that we are not human beings. We are Christ Beings, and this universal law has always been true." Robert nodded, his blue eyes deepening. "We are waking up in Heaven. And when fully aware, we will see that the life we thought we had lived was merely a script we wrote before birth. The Holy Spirit, God's second creation after us, was manifested to heal our magnificent mind because we believed we had separated ourselves from I AM." The librarian, now Ahnora, in the way that names no longer mattered, inhaled sharply. "I finally understand. My family's car accident, their passing, it was something I scripted to understand the immense grief I believed I felt when I thought I had rebelled against God. But now I see. Loss is impossible. Separation is impossible. It has never been God's will, and God's will is all there is. We are eternally held within the mind of God." Robert breathed in this shared recognition, the understanding of forgiveness expanding within him. "As we forgive others, we are truly forgiving ourselves for believing we offended Source. I am Love because I was created by Love. You are Love. Everyone is Love. And now I know what we will do for all eternity . We will be taught all that God knows. We will fully step into who we truly are and remember that we are Co-Creators with God, for God's nature is infinite extension and infinite giving. We will create universes because Love's function is to create."

And in that instant, Robert was no longer in the library. He was seated at his dining room table, the lingering remnants of his drug-induced state slowly dissolving. But he knew he must write. He must record everything so that when clarity returns, he will not forget. His hands moved feverishly across the page, capturing truths that transcended the limitations of time. Jesus appeared across the table, his expression holding something close to amusement, but touched with gentle disappointment. Robert, without hesitation, asked, "Why the look?" Jesus chuckled. "I was looking forward to you believing you had become a mule who could drive a car while searching for a fifth of Jack Daniel's because twenty-five beers wouldn't be enough to stop Bob Hall from his inevitable demise due to brain lesions." Robert sighed. "I'm done with the insanity of the ego. I'm only listening to the Holy Spirit now." Jesus, no longer Elton John, leaned forward, his voice soft. "I have been with you since the moment you were born. I have nurtured, protected, and taught you. The Holy Spirit has even condensed time for you because your lessons are complete. Gladimere was supposed to steal from you tomorrow, but this will not happen. You have already forgiven another friend who stole from you in your imagined past. And now, I have wonderful news. Source is going to wake you up very, very soon. You have mastered the lesson I came to teach." Robert held his breath. "What lesson?" A tender smile flickered across Jesus' face. "Some of my final words while dying on the cross were, 'Father, forgive them, for they know not what they do.' I said it not because our Father forgives, for Source knows of nothing to forgive, but for those witnessing my death. I needed to ingrain the beauty of forgiveness in the collective human psyche. I forgave even while being tortured. And you have learned this lesson. You are dreaming, and you will soon awaken."

Robert's voice grew quiet. "What is true Reality like?" Jesus' expression softened, carrying infinite compassion. "I have saved and purified the remembrance of every act of love you have ever given. Every time you aided the needy, forgave without condition, offered kindness, gave beyond what was expected, and extended love, you created something magnificent. You will understand the beauty of these actions in ways beyond comprehension. Colors you have never seen, sounds beyond earthly measure, tastes rich with Divine Essence. The touch of things will alter at will, smells will hold beauty like music. The reunion with friends and loved ones will be without end. You will master flight, embrace creation, and see that the hardships you endured were mere ripples in a forgotten dream. And all false emotions, loss, worry, anxiety, fear, will be no more. Because they never truly existed." Jesus grinned, eyes glimmering with humor. "And I look forward to your antics in Heaven. You'll be a hilarious stand-up comedian. You have survived time with absolutely zero common sense. Your brothers and sisters will be amazed." Robert gazed at the empty chair where Jesus had sat. He reached for his pen, writing everything before sleep overtook him. He awoke twelve hours later. His writings lay before him, cryptic scrawls, incomprehensible to his waking mind. The experience was missing from his memory, the details blurred into nothingness. He knew he had learned something profound, something eternal . But now, it is gone. Still, he understood. The truth remained in his subconscious, forever imprinted. For some reason, he thought about Peru, about the Shamans, about Ayahuasca. He entertained the notion of recording his next journey, to document truths in a way the world could understand. Then the alarm clock rang, signaling the start of his ordinary workday. Bob, who was once Robert, stirred from his bed. A distant, half-forgotten dream lingered in his mind, something about a library. Something important. But all he could remember now was that he needed to return an overdue book.

## Chapter 3: The Essay Flow

Bob changes his name to Wentworth because his ego demands awe and respect from others. The intense drug experience that follows is based on a real event when, at 28, I overdosed on uncut PCP. While Wentworth's actions may read as humorous, the underlying reality is far from amusing, he is consumed by the most intense fear he has ever known. His mind spins into a relentless cycle, a rapid-fire loop of good and bad thoughts clashing against one another. Every hopeful notion is instantly countered with despair, trapping him in a whirlwind of confusion. The critical turning point comes when he asks, "Is God real?" and hears a powerful "YES" resonate within his heart's mind. In that instant, proof of God's Reality unfolds before him, he sees Gladimere speaking with Jesus. The madness gripping his ego begins to loosen. When Jesus tells Wentworth that his true name is Robert, the ego-driven illusion of Wentworth almost completely dissolves. That is why he is referred to as "Bob

Wentworth" when addressing Jesus. Jesus reveals a truth that shakes Robert's perception, he is talking to a tree. The realization dawns: "Bob and Robert are one and the same." This shift is reflected in the text when Robert meets the librarian, marking the final undoing of Wentworth's false identity. The ego is erased, and with its dissolution, Robert steps fully into truth. As Robert explains Jesus' teachings to the librarian, his awakening deepens, he begins to realize that he is Christ, as we all are. All of his writings emerge upon waking, which is why the essay concludes with the alarm clock ringing at 7:00 AM. What follows is the true account of the long, terrifying, and now-forgotten hours endured under the ego's extreme attack during the overdose on pure PCP. This event, from 1978, is absolutely true.

## Chapter 4: My Horrifying & Catatonic Drug Experience

I had two days off work and a friend, Joe, asked if I would be interested in buying an ounce of pure PCP from the chemist who synthesized it. I discovered after the fact this is a horse tranquilizer sometimes cut with embalming fluid. Sure, why not? I had no idea. After what occurred over the coming days, I could say this. Comparing LSD to PCP, LSD is a shot of beer, and PCP is a fifth of whiskey. PCP is one of the most shockingly horrible drugs in the world. I'm driving back to my apartment, Joe is sitting next to me. He snorted a big line. Instantly, he said, "Hallsey", my nickname, "Where are we going ?" "Back to my apartment." "Where?" "Back to my apartment." "Hallsey, where are we going?" " Back to my apartment." "Where is my dad?" "I don't know, Joe". He went quiet. Wow! I was dating a lady named JoJo. I went into the apartment and told her this stuff was very powerful. We both snorted a very small line. Instantly, everything went euphoric. Surrounded by white light. After a half hour, I wondered where Joe was. I went out to the car, he was drenched in sweat. He hadn't been able to open the door and said he had been out in the universe. He crawled across the street, on all fours, and had urinated himself. He came into the apartment and straight armed my oak coffee table straight over his head. Unbelievable strength. Then both JoJo and Joe were gone. What? Over the next two days, I'm snorting a little every four hours or so with no sleep. I can handle this, I was very wrong. I went to work Friday morning, so high, I didn't know I was high. I worked in the retail appliance industry at corporate headquarters, which also had a sales floor. I found out that I was going to be promoted to store manager. I was dismissed.

This is *exactly* what happened.

My first customers were two men from a company named Stuart Sandwiches, looking to buy a used sixty-nine-dollar freezer. We had an open-to-buy list, where customers with a good buying history could take the product and pay later. I had looked at the wrong list and naturally didn't see the name. I walked upstairs into the vice president's office, which I had never done before. He was in the middle of a meeting and I explained the situation. I told him there was a *man* named Stuart Sandwiches. *It's a company.* He asked me to not let them take it. I went back down, told them, and they went ballistic. I just stood there, looking at the floor. A fellow salesman came over and peacefully resolved the situation. I went and sat at my desk and opened a King James Bible my mother had given me. The words became extremely "pornographic", vial, threatening and menacing. I closed the Bible. A couple of minutes later, there was a man behind me, looking at a stereo. It turns out he was a semi-driver taking a load of appliances back to Bellaire, which was five minutes from my hometown, Martins Ferry. We were also a distribution center. I went back to my desk, tore the front page out of the Bible, and wrote, "Mom, just thinking of you, have a wonderful day. Love, Bob". She had, what turned out to be, terminal breast cancer. I went back to the warehouse, found the driver, and asked if he would mind taking this to my mother in Martins Ferry. He said sure and asked if the semi could maneuver in the backstreets. I looked at the truck, it was miles long. I proceeded to walk back to the sales floor, the driver following me. We were in a darker area of the warehouse when he stopped me, grabbed my hand and explained he was gay, and asked if he could give me oral sex. I have no issues with gay men, however, in my mind, at that moment, I had just given him a "Holy Mission", taking the note to my Mother with cancer. I looked at him, turned around, and went completely insane.

I went to the sales floor and started switching all the price tags. I had an Amana ice and water refrigerator, priced at seventy-nine dollars. A basic washer was over two thousand, a microwave at fifteen hundred and a dishwasher at twenty-nine. There were several customers on the sales floor. I then picked up a can of Coca-Cola, went upstairs, and poured it into an industrial laser printer. I squirted some mustard on my suit and went down and sat at my desk. The V.P. came down a few minutes later and asked, "Bob, What's going on?" Quiet. "Are you drinking anything?" "No." "Are you smoking anything?" "No." I said, "Fred, I'm scared." "Why are you scared?" I told him the truth, that I was overdosing on PCP. About five minutes later, the police arrived and took me to an emergency room. They observed me for quite some time. I have no idea how long because I was lost in the madness of my mind. I was perfectly quiet, the doctor gave me a card to a mental institution, explaining that because I was not violent, I could leave. Somebody drove me back over to work, where I was asked to take the weekend off. I was let go on Monday. A good friend said the printer would randomly print, "Things go better with Coke."

I had a 1969 Chevelle SS. and started driving, I swear I remember hitting one hundred mph. I was not on the interstate, I had no idea where I was and became lost several times. I'm somehow on the interstate, then side roads, back on the interstate. I'm dripping wet from sweat. I ran many red lights and stop signs, all at a very high speed. Somehow, I made it home. Arriving safely without even a ticket qualifies as a miracle. I was blown out of my mind. At this moment, I thought I should call my mother and explain that a gay man might be pulling up in a semi-truck with the front page of the Bible she had given me. Today this seems hilarious. She asked what on earth was wrong with me. I told her the truth, that I was overdosing on PCP, and that I thought I had just lost my job. "You son of a b_itch" and slammed the phone. I had just lost my best friend. I went to hell.

I'm completely insane and under the influence of massive quantities of pure uncut PCP. The summer heat was stifling at over 100 degrees. I'm sitting on the front porch drinking a Little King beer. At this moment, my next-door neighbor, who I had never spoken with for the year I had lived there, came over, sat down, and introduced himself. I looked at him and he transformed. His eyes became black, he grew over ten feet tall with wings and hooves. I said I was sick and had to go inside. I locked the door, took off all my clothes, went to bed and entered hell. All this occurred on a Friday, I came to sanity on Sunday morning. All I can explain about those lost twenty-four hours is that there was no concept of time. I'm visualizing spiders, snakes, bats with human heads, smelling sulfur, seeing humans on fire in agony, lakes of fire, hearing intense screaming, at times in utter blackness. For every good thought, there was an immediate bad thought. My mind was in a continuous loop. Good, bad, good, bad, good, bad. Extremely fast. The fear and pure terror was astoundingly powerful, as I believed I'd be there. Forever. I looked at the clock and the time was 6:01. After thinking countless hours had gone by, I looked again and was terrified to see 6:02, one minute. I remember during those lost twenty-four hours, focusing on a small constant light and breathing, while all this hell was going on around me. I truly believed, if I stopped breathing, I would be in hell. Forever. I woke up on Sunday morning, and the first sound I heard was singing birds. I took the PCP and flushed it. I didn't even smoke weed over the next year or so. Before continuing, I should explain what I know is true. Our eternal Source did not put me through this experience. Source was the light I concentrated on with my right mind and Spirit. What I experienced was an extreme attack by the insanity of my ego. God does not send us trials, as Our Father isn't even aware of this dream universe and has given each the Holy Spirit to heal. All works out for the good of all parties concerned, always. You may not think so at the time. Looking back at my own life, for me, this is very true. "You can't always get what you want, but if you try sometimes, you just might find, you get what you need." The Rolling Stones.

I explained this to a doctor several years later. He told me he was writing a book about the effects of natural hallucinogens on the human psyche. There are many plants that are known to have hallucinogenic properties. These plants contain chemical compounds that can react with the human body in specific ways, affecting the brain and mental state of those who ingest them. He asked if it was pure PCP. I said yes. For some reason, he asked if I was spiritual, and I told him I was Christian. He explained that I had gone catatonic. He had patients who were in mental institutions. Put their hand up, it stays up until you put it down. Their mind is in a good/bad loop. Most came out of it, a few hadn't. PCP "short circuits" the synapse in the brain. The doctor said I had experienced a miracle for not being a living vegetable. Yes, I had. I had been attending church regularly. Believing strongly in the existence of Heaven and hell. Until I became a student of "A Course In Miracles", I still believed in hell because I had seen and experienced it. My mind made the whole exposure up. I now understand the power of our mind.

## Chapter 5: Drug Misinformation

There have never been any deaths associated with LSD toxicity. In other words, no one has ever died from an LSD overdose. As I mentioned, I have never advocated anyone to take the drug. That being said, I will offer my personal experiences. I have tripped hundreds of times and never taken it with anyone. For me, it has always been a very rewarding spiritual high, and I always said a prayer before ingesting it. From an economic standpoint, it is extremely cheap. For $5.00 the high lasts about 8 hours. When in a controlled setting, like being at home listening to favorite music, the sensations are wonderful. Imagine sound turning to color, beautiful patterns and shapes appearing in everything you look upon. I would truly experience a blissful state that was incredible. When it was legal, the military gave it to volunteers to see if their performance improved. That didn't work, people would end up singing in trees, smiling constantly or looking at the stars and universe.

The following is from the Microsoft Bing search engine. "LSD is a popular psychedelic drug that alters the state of your mind in significant ways. This potent drug binds to specific brain cell receptors and alters how the brain responds to serotonin, a neurotransmitter that regulates emotions, moods, and perceptions. By binding to these receptors, LSD modifies neural pathways, producing visual hallucinations and altering the perception of things such as sound and time. Microdosing LSD involves taking a very small dose of the substance, usually around 5–10% of the amount necessary to induce psychoactive effects. Advocates of LSD microdosing claim that the practice has numerous health benefits, such as improving cognition and mood, reducing pain, and helping to treat depression and addiction. Some preliminary research and anecdotal evidence suggest that microdosing LSD may have numerous benefits. These include the ability to enhance cognitive processes and abilities, increase energy levels, improve emotional balance and mood, reduce anxiety, help treat depression, and help treat addiction and reduce substance misuse.

LSD was first synthesized by the Swiss chemist Albert Hofmann in November 1938, while working at the Sandoz laboratories in Basel, Switzerland. Hofmann initially created and studied various lysergic acid derivatives before synthesizing LSD. His original intention was to develop a respiratory and circulatory stimulant (an analeptic) without effects on the uterus, similar to another compound called nikethamide. However, it wasn't until April 19, 1943, that Hofmann accidentally absorbed a small amount of LSD during a re-synthesis and discovered its powerful hallucinogenic effects. In summary, Albert Hofmann's accidental encounter with LSD led to the discovery of its psychedelic properties, forever altering our understanding of consciousness and perception. Physical Safety:Direct toxicity: Unlike some other drugs, LSD itself is not considered highly toxic. There is no known lethal dose of LSD. Accidental harm: However, accidents can occur due to impaired judgment and altered perception while under the influence of LSD. For example, someone might engage in risky behavior or experience accidents. Impurities: Street LSD may contain impurities or other substances, which could pose risks. Psychological Effects: Bad trips: LSD can induce intense anxiety, panic, and paranoia. A "bad trip" can lead to dangerous behavior or self-harm. Flashbacks: Some users experience hallucinogen persisting perception disorder (HPPD), where they have visual disturbances even after the drug has worn off. Pre-existing Conditions: Individuals with pre-existing mental health conditions (such as schizophrenia or bipolar disorder) may be more vulnerable to adverse effects. Suicide risk: While LSD itself doesn't directly cause suicide, it can exacerbate existing mental health issues. Rare Fatalities:Accidental deaths: There have been cases of people accidentally harming themselves while under the influence of LSD (e.g., falling from heights, drowning). Indirect causes: Some fatalities are indirectly related to LSD use, such as accidents during a trip or risky behavior. Unpredictable reactions: Individual reactions to LSD vary, and some people may have severe adverse reactions. Overall Risk: Relative safety: Considering the millions of doses of LSD consumed over decades, the overall risk of death is low. Responsible use: Responsible use, proper set (mindset), and setting (environment) are crucial to minimizing risks." As mentioned, I have never experienced a bad trip and there have been no flashbacks. Simply do what you enjoy, be in the company of friends, play chess or listen to great music. The visuals and sounds are quite extraordinary. If you are at all hesitant, do not take LSD.

CHAPTER 45

# Our Insane World

UNDERSTANDING THE MADNESS OF the world is often the first step toward clarity. It is no wonder that we are witnessing a surge in alcohol and opiate abuse. Since the COVID-19 pandemic, countless people have lost their jobs, supply chain disruptions have driven up the cost of essential goods, and the traditional family structure has been pushed to its limits. Many parents must work just to survive, leaving their children to navigate life on their own. Meanwhile, the prison population continues to climb as the judicial system, fueled by profit, perpetuates cycles of incarceration. Political corruption remains unchecked, with dishonest individuals escaping accountability. The suicide rate has soared as many have lost all sense of hope. A wise friend once shared that the true definition of hell is seeing no hope anywhere, and for many, that sentiment rings painfully true. Alcohol and opiates serve as an escape, a way to silence the relentless noise of a troubled mind. Heroin addiction often begins not as a deliberate choice, but with a love for the feeling it brings. Over time, the drug ceases to be about pleasure and instead becomes a necessity, to stave off withdrawal, to feel normal again. The rise in crack cocaine use is tied to the search for that high, that temporary relief from reality. I have witnessed firsthand the agony of heroin withdrawal, the convulsions, cold sweats, nausea, cramps, and unbearable flu-like symptoms. Those in its grip often wish for death rather than endure its torment. Yet even that pales in comparison to the dangers of alcohol withdrawal. A severe alcoholic, if they quit abruptly, can die from the withdrawal alone.

My writings, or rather our collective expressions, serve a greater purpose: to offer hope. When one truly grasps and internalizes these profound truths, not only does hope begin to take root, but an immense joy follows. This is not a distant promise or abstract concept, it is something I have experienced myself.

CHAPTER 46

# We Are Of One Mind

OUR PERCEPTIONS OF REALITY can often distort the truth, creating illusions that feel overwhelmingly real and terrifying. In moments of fear, we may forget that healing and peace are always within reach, found through the simple act of forgiveness. It is never my intention to persuade anyone that their experience is not real, that would be unkind and unnecessary. Instead, I choose to share the power of forgiveness and invite others to join me in healing our minds together. When I witness the pain of another, whether physical or emotional, I recognize that I too have momentarily lost sight of their perfection and my own. In such moments, we both require healing, and miracles arise when they are shared between souls. This is because, in truth, we are already united within the Wholeness and Oneness of God. Through this shared unity, healing becomes a mutual experience, when one is healed, so is the other.

Because we exist within Unity, Wholeness, and Oneness, separation from each other or from God is impossible. The power of unity far surpasses anything the illusion of ego can create. In the presence of Divine Love, fear dissolves naturally. The only strength the ego possesses is the power we grant it by engaging with its illusions and denying the truth. When we align our minds with ego-based thinking, we fuel its fire, yet it remains inherently powerless. The ego, in reality, does not exist, it is merely an imagined construct. Again, as Jesus teaches in The Course, "By giving power to nothing, he throws away the joyous opportunity to learn that nothing has no power." No matter how intricately the ego disguises its deceptions, nothing will ever amount to more than nothing. As we extend forgiveness, illusions fade, revealing that they were never truly present. They are simply distortions born of fear, created by the thinking mind trapped within the ego's framework. Only through forgiveness can we pierce the veil of deception and recognize that, in truth, there is nothing *to* forgive. Forgiveness allows us to see beyond illusions and perceive what has always been present, the boundless Love of God. Jesus speaks of forgiveness in ACIM with clarity, "Forgiveness recognizes what you thought your brother did to you has not occurred. It does not pardon sins and make them real. It sees there was no sin. And in that view are all your sins forgiven. What is sin, except a false idea about God's Son? Forgiveness merely sees its falsity, and therefore lets it go. What then is free to take its place is now the Will of God."

I often envision God watching over us like a loving parent observing a sleeping child. The parent does not experience the content of the child's dreams, only the restless movements, the tossing and turning that signal distress. Yet, the parent does not attempt to resolve the imagined conflicts within the dream, for they know it is not real and cannot harm the child. The parent simply waits for the child to awaken, to recognize that the nightmare was never real. This is the wish of our Father, that we awaken from our illusions and remember that we have never truly left our eternal Home. We remain safe, embraced within the arms of Divine Love.

CHAPTER 47

# The Beautiful Laws Of God

When we entertained the fleeting thought of separation from God, we shifted from knowing to perceiving. The realm of perception, unlike truth, is interpretative, dualistic, linear, and illusory. It reflects everything that truth is not. In truth, we are undoing what never truly existed. We are dissolving the belief in separation, transcending the idea of fragmentation, revealing Reality as it has always been, unchanged and whole. The laws of perception reflect what we choose to believe. These beliefs shape our deepest despair or our highest aspirations. Whatever we place our faith in becomes our lived experience. Perception mirrors either a peaceful mind or a tormented one, and the choice is ours to make. A happy dream arises from right-mindedness. It is the result of mindfulness and presence, of choosing Life, Love, Joy, and Peace consistently. The strength of our faith in these choices bears fruit in the way our lives unfold. Through forgiveness, we release anything that denies truth, and as we do, we witness Heaven's reflection taking shape before us. No longer victims of perception, we become witnesses to the Laws of Love, seeing God in all that we perceive. Faith is never lacking; we all have faith in something, whether it be truth or illusions. As we grow in awareness, we can detect the ego's distortions before they take hold. With peace as our constant choice, peace becomes our natural state. Any deviation from peace feels like a pebble in our shoe, a reminder to choose again. Choosing again begins with recognizing a disturbance in our peace. I bring my mind to stillness, abandoning thought and inner dialogue, allowing whatever arises to simply be. In this state, I observe rather than engage. If fear appears, I let it wash over me while holding my awareness of God, anchored in truth, present in the Now. Non-resistance is key; rather than struggling against negativity, I allow it to pass through me, flowing until it dissipates. Resistance only holds pain in place. By letting it be, I let it go. In truth, it is not I who releases it, it releases me. What is not real has no power unless I grant it power. Darkness vanishes in the presence of light.

Our willingness to choose again activates the higher mind, the Holy Spirit, initiating the correction of wrong-mindedness into right-mindedness. This transformation is Heaven's reflection. We step into it naturally as life unfolds before us. At the level of mind, there is nothing to do, only to be present, to rest in stillness and quiet. As we take each step, God walks with us, straightening the distortions created by the ego. Right-mindedness brings clarity, certainty, and peace. This stillness always welcomes us, inviting us to accept it fully. It is not an action, but a state of Being. The path forward will vary from one individual to another, differing in means but not in purpose. A Holy Relationship serves to accelerate healing and save time. One moment spent in true connection with another restores the universe for both. You are prepared. Now you need only to remember that there is nothing you must do. When peace finally settles upon those who have struggled with temptation and resisted the pull of sin; when light at last enters the contemplative mind; when the goal is finally reached, this realization arrives with quiet certainty: "I need do nothing." Reality provides all that is necessary. The ego will attempt to disrupt this understanding, casting doubt and arguing its case. It believes itself wiser than God. Yet beyond its frantic assertions, Reality remains as it always has, unchanged and ever-present. It waits patiently for us to notice, to embrace, and to accept its grace. Love's reflection continues to illuminate the way, guiding us home to our unity with God and one another. In Peace, we will listen to angels. In truth, we will see the sky adorned with shimmering diamonds.

CHAPTER 48

# The Tender Commandments

NOW THAT WE HAVE explored certain Biblical passages and their deeper significance, let us turn our attention to the Ten Commandments. According to the Bible, these were given to Moses by God on Mount Sinai. Whether this account is historically accurate is ultimately irrelevant; what truly matters is whether we choose to follow their wisdom. There is no divine judgment if we choose otherwise, for these commandments were placed into human consciousness for our benefit, not as a tool for punishment. When viewed as guidance rather than law, they offer a framework for living a life aligned with integrity and inner peace.

I. You shall have no other gods before Me.

*By far the greatest idol is sex.* First off, there is absolutely nothing wrong with sex. The act is very natural and is designed for the pro-creation of life and as normal as eating. I've never heard anybody say, "My orgasm was horrible." I've known several who are obsessed with sex, both male and female. My friend's dad is my age and spent over $25,000 last year on porn sites and fantasy hook-ups. He finally went to counseling as he was almost homeless. This is the ego's hardest hitting artillery to keep us locked in the body. *Money is a close second.* We work all of our lives to accumulate a bunch of stuff. Where does all this end up? Normally in garage sales or landfills. I have a few friends who are extremely wealthy and completely miserable. One has spent thousands upon thousands on elaborate security systems due to his extreme paranoia that he'll be robbed. I certainly admit it's better to have money than not. *Drugs.* I've gone over seven days with no food, this is not pleasant. At that time, I was living with two close friends who were addicted to the worst opiate there is. Heroin. I'd never touched the stuff because of watching what they went through, shooting up every morning and evening. Being dope sick is much worse than having the flu. Convulsions, diarrhea, vomiting and being unable to sleep. I was an enabler who couldn't stand watching them go through such misery. From experience, all addicts start down this road because initially the numbing feeling is ecstatic. However, all will reach the point where they require the needle just to feel normal. The reason we're witnessing the explosion of crack cocaine is this is their preferred method to get high. The only thing worse than getting off opiates is alcohol. Addicts want to die, true alcoholics will. *Food is another idol.* Ever notice how many are obese? When we eat, our brain releases certain chemicals like dopamine and serotonin, which are associated with feelings of pleasure and well-being. These chemicals reinforce the act of eating, making it an enjoyable experience. However, the pleasure quickly fades and the obese need more and more and more. An ego tactic of pleasure quickly turning to misery. *Sports comes to mind.* Football, basketball, soccer, golf and numerous other events have some completely obsessed. Marriages have ended in divorce because all communication stopped. *Television must be way up on the list.* How many spend countless hours watching strictly as an escape? Periodically, I'll glimpse at the tube and am still amazed at how idiotic it is. Back in the early 1960s, tests were performed at outside movie drive-ins. One picture frame would flash of a beautiful sunrise, then another of pop-corn, another of the ocean and quickly a picture of a hot dog. The frames were so fast that the eye couldn't see, but the mind did. There was a very substantial increase in food sales. This is called subliminal advertising and is considered extremely deceptive by the Federal Trade Commission. However, it's still practiced in a slower form. Ever notice how fast commercials change scenes? The reason being is this keeps your attention. I very much enjoy movies, and this is all I ever watch. *Gambling is also a big idol.* There are numerous others, but you get the general idea. These gods offer nothing but potential misery.

II. You shall not make for yourself a carved image.

Ancient Pagan Religions: Many ancient civilizations, such as the Egyptians, Greeks, and Romans, created statues and images of their gods and goddesses, which they worshiped. Golden Calf Incident: In the Bible, the Israelites created a golden calf to worship while Moses was receiving the Ten Commandments on Mount Sinai. This event is a direct example of disobeying the commandment. Hindu Idolatry: In Hinduism, there are various deities, and idols are often created as physical representations of these gods. Devotees perform rituals and prayers in front of these idols. Buddhist Statues: In Buddhism, statues of the Buddha are commonly made and venerated. Although these are intended to be reminders of the Buddha's teachings, they can be seen as contrary to the commandment. These are all examples of the total insanity of our ego, let's all pray to the holy ashtray.

III. You shall not take the name of the Lord your God in vain.

God's Biblical name is Yahweh (Jehovah) in Islam it's Allah. Several other names are Elohim, Adonai, ABBA, and Brahman. Over the years, I've heard numerous statements like, "God dammit, that man blaring his car horn is an idiot." Remember that God is a title, like man is a title. In other words, "Man dammit, that woman holding up the line is inconsiderate." means the same thing. The thought occurred to me that the name most mentioned by all of humanity is Jesus Christ. Somebody hits their thumb with a hammer, "Jesus Christ, that hurt." What exactly does taking in vain mean? Having a feeling of no respect. Do you honestly feel that God cares the slightest if you believe in Him or not? Does this affect Source negatively? Of course not, the only one you're hurting is yourself. Again, thank you, ego. Once we've totally understood the concept that God Is and after reading about the glory of Heaven, shouldn't we feel the deepest Love, respect, awe, and admiration? By honoring God's name, individuals are reminded of their relationship with the Divine and their commitment to living a life of faith.

IV. Remember the Sabbath day, to keep it holy.

At its core, this commandment invites rest. After a long week of work, setting aside time for relaxation and connection is essential. Families often observe the Sabbath through shared meals, outdoor activities, and meaningful interactions. It is a reminder to pause, appreciate life, and nurture relationships.

V. Honor your father and your mother.

My parents were old enough to be my grandparents, so this was always very easy. I'll explain a little story. Dad was superintendent at Wheeling Pittsburgh Steel, being boss over the nail mill at LaBelle and the coupling department at Benwood. He had a trait that is somewhat missing today, integrity. If he told you he'd do something, he did it. He *always* kept his word. I've lived by his standard all my life and am thankful dad taught me this. When I was 18, he hired me to run a reamer. I started on the midnight Saturday shift. A coupling was threaded on both sides and held the pipe together. The reamer is a big drill bit. A coupling would go into a vice grip, the drill would come down and thread one side. I'd pull the vice out, turn it over, push it back in and thread the other side. Knock the coupling out and do another. I worked hard all night and was absolutely exhausted in the morning. I turned the car on and couldn't hear the engine running due to my ringing ears. I was filthy dirty, covered in cutting oil and *furious*. When I arrived home, dad was sitting in his living room chair drinking coffee. I tearfully said," There's nothing you can say, nothing you can do. I am *not* going back to that hellhole." Now, it's important to him that I work hard, he's the big boss and all the men knew I was his son. His response was," Bob, you're 18 and a man. Your mother and I are going on vacation today, and we won't know if you will go back in or not, your call." If he'd said *anything* else, I would have quit. I went to work and became quite good on the job. I maintain to this day, if I hadn't, I would have been a quitter all my life. What if the parents are abusive and demanding? At least you're being taught what you do not want. This is a wonderful opportunity to practice forgiveness, for if you can forgive a horrible life as a child, you'll be able to forgive anything.

VI. You shall not murder.

This commandment is straightforward, not only does taking a life violate moral principles, but it also leads to lifelong consequences, including imprisonment.

VII. You shall not commit adultery.

Years before Mary Jo's passing, I worked as a general store manager for a large retail appliance company. One afternoon, I was speaking with Tom, one of our top salesmen. He was confident and charismatic, proudly recounting his latest romantic encounters. As Mary Jo approached, he suddenly exclaimed, "OMG, look at her body." I replied, "Thank you." He hesitated. "Why?" "That's my wife." Tom's expression shifted instantly. "Oh, Bob, I am so sorry." "There's no need to apologize, you just gave me a compliment." He was visibly shaken as I introduced them, his former bravado replaced with discomfort. That brief exchange highlighted the nature of jealousy and insecurity, powerful emotions that can destroy relationships. Jealousy is rooted in fear, the irrational belief that another person can take away the one we love. It is, at its core, an attack on oneself, an admission of insecurity, a lack of trust. Mary Jo and I never struggled with jealousy. We had built a solid foundation of trust through shared experiences, deep love, and commitment to our children. People always noticed her, drawn not only to her physical beauty but also to her warmth and spiritual radiance. She carried herself with confidence and kindness, making everyone feel valued. Our love was secure, unwavering, and built on mutual respect. To preserve such a bond, faithfulness is essential.

VIII. You shall not steal.

The lesson of honesty struck me early in life. When I was nine years old, I stole a pack of firecrackers while visiting a friend on the Fourth of July. My mother discovered the theft and insisted I return them, along with $5 from my allowance. I had never felt such embarrassment. That experience left a lasting impression, I swore to never steal again, a promise I have kept to this day. Beyond morality, honoring this principle keeps one from facing serious legal consequences.

IX. You shall not bear false witness against your neighbor.

Lying creates unnecessary complications. A simple truth is easier to maintain than a web of deception. If an issue arises between neighbors, the best approach is direct communication. Gossip and misrepresentation only deepen conflicts. During my time as a store manager, I oversaw eighty employees. Before our grand opening, I gathered everyone for a meeting focused on morale. I shared my philosophy, explaining that poor workplace culture leads to declining performance. I urged employees to communicate openly rather than vent their frustrations to third parties. "If Bill has a problem with Sue," I said, "Don't go to Fred and talk about Sue. Go directly to Sue. If you can't resolve the issue, come to me in confidence, behind closed doors, and we'll work through it together." This approach strengthened our team. Over time, a few employees sought private meetings, and each conflict was resolved. By fostering direct dialogue and mutual understanding, we built an environment where people felt comfortable working together. As a result, our store exceeded sales expectations, thriving because employees genuinely enjoyed coming to work.

X. You shall not covet.

Coveting, desiring what belongs to another, is a destructive force. Over twenty-five years ago, I wrestled with jealousy over my best friend Dave's financial success. As a self-made millionaire, he achieved a level of prosperity that seemed unattainable to me. That envy weighed on me for years, a silent burden. However, as time passed, my perspective shifted. When Dave spoke of his latest financial endeavors, I no longer felt resentment, I felt sincere happiness for him. That change brought relief. Envy had been exhausting, but genuine joy for others was liberating. Ultimately, the Ten Commandments were designed not as restrictions, but as guidance to help us live with integrity and peace. Their purpose is not to serve God's needs but to benefit humanity, offering wisdom that shapes our interactions and choices.

CHAPTER 49

# A Friend's Thoughts

THE NATURE OF LOVE, as described here, transcends the illusions of perception. Love is not an action, an exchange, or something to be grasped, it simply is. In truth, Love exists beyond form, beyond ego, beyond projection. It is not entwined with neediness, fear, or dependency, nor is it something we give to receive. Instead, love is our essence, our state of being, untouched by illusion. Every loving thought we hold is eternal, a reflection of Divine Truth. Though we may perceive these thoughts within the framework of separation, they remain real because love is real. The illusion of separation clouds this understanding, yet through forgiveness, we clear away distortions, allowing love to be recognized in its purity. Forgiveness, then, becomes the means by which the past is transformed, no longer a conflict with the present but an extension of reality.

The Holy Spirit facilitates this transformation, bringing love into relationships that seem rooted in separation. Where once there was conflict, resentment, or fear, love emerges, reshaped, redeemed, and untainted by illusion. Atonement focuses on the past, for it is within the memory of separation that healing must occur. The moment we release our attachment to separation, we step into truth, where love has always existed, unwavering and whole.

The ego's version of love is not love at all, it is attachment, possession, and a desperate attempt to fill an internal void. It is manipulation disguised as affection, a cycle of neediness and dependency masquerading as connection. When we identify with the ego, we see others as bodies, as separate entities that we can use to alleviate the discomfort of our own fractured sense of self. This leads to a mind trapped between two states, the wrong (personal) mind and the right (Holy Spirit) mind, constantly shifting between illusion and truth. When rooted in the wrong mind, love becomes distorted into fear, resentment, and control. Yet, no one remains in this state permanently. Moments arise when the ego's incessant voice quiets, when identification with its false narrative ceases. In these moments, love becomes real again, extending effortlessly to others without condition or expectation. It is not the warped version of love we construct within the framework of special relationships but something pure, untouched by illusion.

Ironically, even within the ego's misguided pursuit of validation, there can be moments of awakening. When everything momentarily aligns with the ego's desires, when someone behaves exactly as the ego dictates, the constant internal chatter stops. For an instant, the need-driven mind falls away, and without consciously realizing it, we step into truth. In that silence, in that moment without struggle, we unknowingly touch the hand of the Holy Spirit. We enter a space where love extends naturally, not from demand, but from presence.

While special relationships are built on illusion, love itself is never lost. Jesus teaches that even within the distortions, the genuine spark of love remains and can be purified. The context may be flawed, but the essence of love survives, waiting to be freed from the ego's grip. Love, once stripped of illusion, remains eternal, unchanging, and ever-present. It is not something we must create or seek, it is simply what we are when we let go of everything that is not real.

## CHAPTER 50

# Source Never Leaves Us

SPIRITUAL GROWTH OFTEN EMERGES from moments of deep struggle, inviting us to examine our beliefs and shift our understanding of ourselves and the world. When faced with suffering, we may question why such trials exist, but through reflection, we recognize that adversity is not punishment, it is an opportunity to awaken to a greater truth. The power of God within us far surpasses any temporary influence wielded in the world. No matter how circumstances may appear, Divine Love remains unshaken, extending infinitely beyond the illusions of control and separation. The journey to awakening is long, sometimes spanning lifetimes, yet every soul will ultimately return to truth. There is no eternal damnation, no place of punishment, only the unfolding process of remembering our unity with God. Through challenges and loss, we grow in understanding. Looking back, we may see that our greatest periods of spiritual transformation occurred during and after times of hardship. Each experience carries a lesson, revealing new depths of wisdom and strength. Pain does not come from God, nor does suffering serve as divine retribution. Instead, God is the unwavering Presence that helps us rise beyond difficulty, guiding us toward healing and expansion. The manuscripts I write serve to illuminate these truths, to help others recognize the meaning behind life's struggles and the deeper purpose within each circumstance. What we perceive as setbacks are often stepping stones leading us closer to awakening. True Divinity is not vengeful, wrathful, or jealous, but an endless Source of Love, guiding us ever forward.

CHAPTER 51

# The Highest Fatality Rate Plant In The Nation

AFTER GRADUATING FROM COLLEGE, I accepted a position as a floor foreman at Buckeye Steel Castings in Columbus, overseeing the midnight shift and managing the pouring of five thirty-ton heats of molten steel each night. The job came through an employment agency, but after my first shift, I was convinced I couldn't continue. When I returned to the agency, they reminded me of the contract I had signed. If I didn't stay for at least three months, I would owe an $800 fee and be left without a job. With little choice, I returned and remained there for four years. Buckeye Steel Castings was known for being one of the most dangerous industrial facilities in the country, its high fatality rate a testament to outdated infrastructure and hazardous conditions. Built in the late 1800s, long before regulatory commissions enforced safety measures, the foundry was a harsh, unforgiving environment. Many workers bore physical scars from the steel, the loss of limbs, severe burns, and permanent injuries were common. My own body carries reminders of those years: a metal plate in my left leg, a bolt through my hip, and large burn scars on my hip and arm. Three years into my tenure, I experienced a moment that would forever redefine the way I perceived fate and miracles. Management had temporarily reassigned me to oversee the mold master, a machine that produced smaller steel castings for the railroad industry. Among our many products were couplers, frames, axle housings, and bolsters, with our largest casting being a fifty-ton pipe cap used in offshore oil drilling. The casting process relied on facing sand, which captured precise impressions before molten steel was poured into the molds. The sand was produced in maulers, located nearly a fifth of a mile away from the mold master. It was then transported via a three-story-high conveyor belt, moving continuously toward its final destination. Upon arrival, a plow directed the sand into a chute, where it would drop three stories into the molding equipment.

That day, the plow jammed in the up position, halting production. With maintenance occupied elsewhere, I decided to fix the issue myself. Climbing three stories up to the catwalk, I examined the air valve and released the jam with a screwdriver. Once the machine resumed operation, I walked the long distance to check if the sand was being made properly. What happened next was the result of a single, careless mistake. The overhead cranes operated on two parallel railroad tracks, one on the south side and the other on the north. These cranes, powered by immense fifty-thousand-horsepower engines, lifted ladles of molten steel with massive pulleys and hooks. To prevent damage in case of collisions, they were equipped with long bumpers. Standing on the catwalk, I impulsively sat on the railroad track to get a better view of the maulers. A quick glance at the crane operator's cab thirty yards away convinced me it was empty. In reality, the operator had been bending down, out of sight. Wearing safety glasses limited my peripheral vision, preventing me from noticing the danger approaching. In a split second, the crane's bumper slammed into me, trapping me beneath its force. The operator, looking at the floor, caught a glimpse of my extended leg just in time. Reacting instantly, he halted the crane. However, a thirty-ton machine does not stop immediately, the momentum carries it forward, creating a dangerous drift. Had he hesitated even a fraction of a second longer, I would have been torn in half. The bumper struck and released in a moment's time, snapping my left femur in two. The pain sent me into immediate shock, and I lost consciousness. What stayed with me long after the injury was not just the trauma, but the undeniable miracle of survival. The operator had no reason to expect someone to be in that location, yet he saw my leg in a fleeting instant. His swift reaction saved my life. That single act, made in mere seconds, spared me from an irreversible fate. In an environment where danger was ever-present, this was a miracle of the highest order.

# THE HIGHEST FATALITY RATE PLANT IN THE NATION

## CHAPTER 52

# Our Tragic Second Honeymoon

We'd say, "One week closer". Mary Jo was forty-three, an exceptional employee at Time Warner Cable, selling commercials with a skill that set her apart. In just one year, she became the top representative in the Pittsburgh district, earning, not winning, an all-expense-paid, five-day cruise on Carnival. As the time approached, we spent Saturday at the mall, picking up last-minute essentials. While walking, Mary Jo suddenly stopped, mesmerized by a painting by Thomas Kinkade titled "A New Day Dawning." She gazed at it, reflecting for a moment before saying, "I'll bet that's what Heaven looks like." I'm looking at the same painting now. During those days, she would occasionally bring up the subject of death in ways that felt unusual. "I don't know what I would do without you," she had said. I replied, "Honey, me neither." Sunday arrived, and we flew out of Pittsburgh. Mary Jo held onto my arm, resting her head on my shoulder. She had never flown before, and the fear of it had settled in. Upon landing in Florida, we boarded the ship, brimming with excitement. This was our second honeymoon. As the ship set sail for Nassau, we stopped at a small island, strolling through the local vendors' displays. The last item Mary Jo ever purchased was a cross.

That evening, she dressed in a black sequined gown, looking elegantly radiant. After enjoying the Captain's Dinner, we watched a Broadway show, then had our pictures taken, our last. In that final photograph, her hand rested on my heart. Next, we went to a club with a dance floor, sipping champagne, tipping glasses, celebrating a night that felt as magical as the turn of a new year. This was much better than any New Year's Eve. We danced, then sat down. She died.

Mary Jo had complained about a pain in her leg, a fleeting discomfort that didn't seem to warrant alarm. Yet on the dance floor, reality shattered. Her stomach swelled, her body expelling fluid in a terrible, violent final act. The pressure changes from the aircraft had unleashed a blood clot, rupturing her heart instantly. She was gone, and I plunged into incomprehensible disbelief. My mind could not process what my eyes had seen. Time lost all meaning. A doctor appeared, asking questions that barely registered. Was she on drugs? No. Has she ever done drugs? No. Did she have medical conditions? No. How old was she? The weight of everything pressed so hard on my thoughts that I couldn't even recall the exact number. I muttered, "Early forties." I can't remember leaving the dance floor or speaking with the ship's captain. A sedative and nerve pill sent me into a restless sleep in a different cabin, and when I woke, the cabin was hollow, empty, yet Mary Jo's perfume lingered in the air, thick and unmistakable. In a trance, I found myself standing at our door. The strength it took to step inside was something I had never known before. Fear surged through me as I entered. Just yesterday, this room was filled with laughter, with love. Now it stood silent, stripped of everything but the aching absence. I sat down, trying to stave off the dizziness. And then, a realization, love transcends life and death. A peace washed over me, fleeting and fragile. *She was with me.* And still, I trembled. Packing became a slow, agonizing process, every item reminding me of what had just been lost. My body rebelled, collapsing momentarily under the weight of it all. The scent of her perfume grew stronger, suffocating, as though she stood beside me. My blood pressure must have been through the roof, and if not for the sedatives still lingering in my system, I might have fainted. Looking back, it astounds me that I didn't ask for help. But I wasn't thinking logically. I was trapped inside a nightmare, one that refused to release me.

A transoceanic call was arranged. The unbearable task of notifying our children loomed. Tracy, our eldest, was studying optometry at Ohio State. Tara, a high school senior. Travis, only in eighth grade. But I couldn't tell them. Instead, I called Mary Jo's mother, Jewel, one of the strongest souls I had ever met. There was a gasp, then silence, long enough that I feared she might have fainted. The captain later approached me, asking if I remembered our conversation the night before. I did not. He explained that under international law, her body could be left at the next port, Nassau. But if she remained on the ship, she would return to the States on Friday, avoiding bureaucratic complications. I agreed. The arrangements were made, and I flew out of Nassau. At the airport, I watched couples holding hands, their lives intact, their futures certain. None of them understood what I had just endured. On the flight to Pittsburgh, the seat beside me sat empty, a cruel reminder. The grief struck so suddenly that I gasped, my body shaking. And then, inexplicably, warmth spread over me, like the soft break of an egg against my scalp. Peace, but only for a fleeting moment. I knew, without question, that Mary Jo was there, resting her head against my shoulder, just as she had two days before. Jewel understood the gravity of telling Tracy, wisely choosing not to do it over the phone. She enlisted Shane, Tracy's cousin, to drive to Columbus. A half-hour from the apartment, he made the mistake of calling ahead. Tracy, sharp as ever, knew something was wrong. Why would Shane be coming to see her? He told her over the phone. When he arrived, the apartment was in shambles. That half-hour, spent in isolation, was the worst of her life. Our beautiful daughter had faced the unbearable alone.

Our family's autobiography, "Two Faces, One Life: The Journey Within" explains in great detail this time of our life. I will mention, what in retrospect, is an amazing occurrence. I've explained that Dave is my best friend and his wife Robin gifted me with Rebecca Springer's beautiful manuscript. A year before Robin died Dave had called and was sobbing when explaining that she'd been diagnosed with liver cancer. The following fall they had invited me to drive the three hours to their home as Robin wanted to give me a present. Mary Jo couldn't go as she had made arrangements with her sister to help with the upcoming family Labor Day festivities. Explaining to Mary Jo that I didn't want to drive up alone, and I had work to do around the property, I was sitting in the basement when I heard, "Go." Somewhat astounded, I drove with the radio off as I wanted to meditate. The first person I called after arriving home from our tragedy was Dave. He was on business in the Carolinas, and dropped everything, arriving at my side in only two days. He was the only one who said anything that made sense and I still periodically thank him for his advice. Dave explained, "Bob, you're going to go one of two ways. Either you'll make everyone around you miserable because you're drowning in self-pity, or you'll realize nothing will ever happen that can be worse than this and you'll find peace." With the grace of God I went the latter route. What is amazing are the similarities between our lives. Dave and Robin only dated for three months and were married twenty years. Mary Jo and I only dated for three months and were married twenty years. They raised two girls, one boy, one adopted. We raised two girls, one boy, one adopted. Mary Jo was 43 when she died, Robin was 43 when she died. The day that Mary Jo died was Robin's birthday. The odds of these parallels are astronomical, and I view them as a Heavenly message, especially when Robin gave me, "My Dream of Heaven" as she was dying.

# CHAPTER 53

# Paranormal Occurrences

MARY JO HAS VISITED me in dreams, along with extraordinary events that prove, beyond the shadow of a doubt, that miracles are natural occurrences. They exist to affirm the Reality of Heaven. I was living in a single-bedroom apartment at the time. A friend and I had settled in for a Netflix movie with a beer in hand. It was Halloween. The buzzer sounded, someone at the entrance to the building. I answered, but no one responded. Probably trick-or-treaters. A few minutes later, the buzzer rang again. Still no one. The third time, I quickly stepped out, determined to catch sight of whoever was playing games. There was no sign of anyone. We resumed watching the movie when a knock echoed through the door. I opened it. Nothing. The building had no closed doors in the long hallway due to fire codes, and no place for anyone to hide. Minutes later, another knock. This time, I ran. The hallway stretched out empty before me. Ron looked at me, perplexed. "What is going on?" "I have no idea." Another knock, then, the door opened. The second time it happened, I saw the doorknob turn. Inside the apartment stood my oak china cupboard, an antique from our old home. Mary Jo Loved this piece. Its door creaked open. I closed it. It opened again and moved gently, back and forth. Then, the scent of roses filled the air, her favorite flower. My friend smelled nothing. The strange occurrences stopped. We had been paid a visit.

While working at Verizon, I assisted a young woman in her twenties with a phone issue. For some inexplicable reason, I briefly mentioned Mary Jo's passing. Why had I spoken about such a personal matter to a stranger? She nodded. "And the ship made arrangements and flew you out of Nassau?" I stared. "Yes." I had not mentioned this detail. She had been on the same cruise when she was fifteen years old. What were the odds? Years later, I sat with friends and several couples I had never met, drinking beer. The conversation drifted toward death, and detailed discussions emerged. I shared our family's tragedy, and a married couple exchanged glances before speaking. "That was you?" They had been on the same cruise ship a year later. The crew had still been talking about the beautiful woman who had suddenly died on the dance floor while celebrating a second honeymoon. Looking back, these random encounters were messages from Heaven. What other explanation could there possibly be?

I soon tired of telecommunications and interviewed for a position at Hollywood Casino. The idea of becoming a dealer intrigued me, I was a decent poker player but knew little of craps or roulette. I paid three hundred dollars for a twelve-week training course covering blackjack, mini-baccarat, and other table games. After ninety days of employment, the casino reimbursed the fee. The job was excellent, high-paying, with a seven p.m. to two a.m. schedule. I worked there for over two years without ever being late. That summer afternoon, I lay by the pool, the clock reading four-thirty. I worked out for an hour, showered, and drove twenty-five minutes to the casino. Upon arrival, I realized I was an hour late. It was eight o'clock. My first thought was that I had misread the time, but as I dealt cards, the Truth pressed in. For years, my routine had been precise. I had not misread the time. I had lost an hour.

# CHAPTER 54

# The Emmaus Walk

YEARS LATER, AN EXTRAORDINARY miracle unfolded during the Emmaus Walk. I had become close friends with Anora, who lived in North Carolina. We had met on a dating site, talking for countless hours over the past year but never meeting in person. One day, out of the blue, she called and asked if I would attend a three-day church seminar. I had not set foot in a church in years, there had been no reason to. She explained that the retreat was called the Emmaus Walk and that I could only attend if sponsored by someone who had already participated, which she had. Curious, I asked about the name and its purpose. She shared the story of two men traveling toward a town called Emmaus after Jesus had been crucified. A third man joined them, explaining the true meaning of their scriptures, the Old Testament. His wisdom astonished them. When they arrived, they prepared a meal, and the moment they broke bread, their eyes were opened. They realized they had been speaking with Jesus himself. And then, he vanished. She didn't know if the retreat would benefit me but had seen it change lives. I agreed to attend.

On Friday evening, an elderly gentleman picked me up. The church was forty-five minutes west, and as we drove, the sunset bathed the fields in golden light. This was one of the most beautiful sunsets I'd ever witnessed. I asked what people gained from the retreat, and he told me I would learn something, though he had no idea what that might be. Seventeen men had gathered. Our cell phones and watches were collected, we would have no concept of time and would be awakened by the sound of handbells. Some online atheists have suggested the phones were taken to hack them, that stolen identities might explain the following miracles. But I knew better. Years of selling high-ticket merchandise had honed my ability to read people, and the sincerity of these volunteers was unquestionable. The minister explained that members of the church would be in the prayer room interceding for us continually, day and night. Every meal was home-cooked, and requests, no matter how small, like an unavailable Mountain Dew, were met with swift generosity.

Saturday morning, we gathered in a conference room and divided into groups of five. A spokesman was chosen from each. The minister explained that we would hear speakers share their traumatic experiences and how they had survived. Our role was to listen, take notes, and, by Sunday afternoon, share what we had learned. Two speakers left a lasting impression. The first, with tears in his eyes, shared that he had been abused by a priest as a child, years of suffering that still required psychiatric treatment. The second was an elderly man, broad-shouldered and deep-voiced, once the head minister of a large church. His trauma began in his sixties. One Sunday morning, he stood holding a toothbrush but could not recall what it was for. His wife found him sitting on the kitchen floor, crying. He would spend months in therapy for severe clinical depression. Sunday afternoon, our group reflected on what we had learned. A mutual decision was made about what should be shared, and then I spoke. "I've never explained in public what my family endured or how we survived. I'd be honored to do so now."

All agreed. When our turn came, I spoke for twenty minutes, recounting the tragedy of losing Mary Jo and the journey of understanding that followed. The minister and several others shook my hand. I explained that I was simply a messenger, helping others find meaning in personal loss. Two men approached. One was elderly, caring for his wife as she battled cancer. My words, that death is an illusion, and we live forever, had touched him deeply. The other was a young father of three who had lost his job, his unemployment benefits nearly expired. I had shared my belief that worry only robs us of peace, that the ego keeps us trapped in the past or anxious for the future, preventing us from living in the present and speaking to God, Now. He grasped my hand. "I've never heard that before. Thank you." "You're welcome." Truth is truth.

Saturday night, we entered the empty sanctuary where services were held. The space was vast, the communion entirely optional, yet all accepted. Sunday evening, the miracles arrived. We expected the sanctuary to be empty again. But when the doors opened, hundreds of people stood before us, holding candles in reverence for those who had completed the Emmaus Walk. A wave of indescribable love overcame me, like the touches I had felt from Mary Jo after her passing, but deeper. As we took our seats, I saw Anora. The church had paid for her flight from the Carolinas so that we could finally meet, an amazing gift. After the congregation departed, we were advised to take communion once more. This time, we were instructed to place something on the bread that we wished to let go and the bread would be ingested by another. I placed on the bread the lingering grief of losing Mary Jo. I was healed, a miracle.

As we packed, a young man I had met the night before approached. He was married with four children, worked two jobs, and was an exceptional guitarist. "Mary Jo was blonde, right?" "Yes." "And she enjoyed dressing in black?" "Yes." "Who is Travie?" "Our nickname for our son, Travis." "And you have a favorite picture of Mary Jo, you're lying on your back with a baby on your chest. Her name starts with a T. Who is that?" "Tara." I was astonished. "How do you know this?" Mary Jo had come to him in a dream. For those who ask for proof that God exists, here it is. How else could he have known? She also told him she would visit me twice more, which she did. He explained that Mary Jo was proud of how well our children were doing and believed I was fulfilling my role simply by being there for all three. That night, the driver brought Anora and myself back to my apartment, where we talked until dawn as she was also a student of The Course. She flew out the next day, having been, in a way, the author of one of the greatest miracles I had ever witnessed.

CHAPTER 55

# The Most Astounding Experience I'll Ever Have

MARY JO'S LAST VISIT was an experience unlike any other, one that remains imprinted upon my soul. I mentioned this before but due to the flow of my manuscript it needs repeating. Years ago, I conducted extensive research for another writing project, uncovering studies in California and Switzerland on the therapeutic potential of microdosing LSD. The findings were astounding, patients suffering from severe bipolar disorder, deep depression, acute anxiety, and even schizophrenia were experiencing profound relief, some even being cured. LSD interacts with brain receptors, altering how the mind processes serotonin, the neurotransmitter responsible for mood, emotion, and perception. My own relationship with hallucinogens was rooted in personal exploration, never in excess. I never advocated their use, nor do I now. I have not touched psychedelics in over fifteen years, and at this stage of life, I no longer feel the need. But back then, it was a spiritual adventure. Alone with music and the shifting kaleidoscope of perception, I would sit in quiet reverence. Sixteen years ago, I transitioned on LSD every weekend for over a year. It was my own journey, sometimes in solitude, sometimes in the company of friends unaware of my altered state. Those nights were filled with laughter, shared stories, and music. On a Sunday morning, seven old friends from shared festival days sat on the floor of my living room and each took one hit of acid. Jordan advised, "Bob, you need to take ten." She was referring to the original Grateful Dead LSD. I held the strip in my mouth, swallowed, and heard her gasp. "OMG, you took twenty." I had doubled over. An hour passed, and the group sat in a circle, speaking freely. As they talked, their auras vibrated and shifted, colors changing with the ebb and flow of conversation. The experience was mesmerizing. For the first time, I saw people not just speaking, but truly communicating, every question perfectly understood, every answer seamlessly given. They spoke of childhood memories, life's trials, joyful discoveries, lost loves, and deep regrets. They shared tales of dancing, drum circles, dreams, harrowing moments, and the visions that guided them through darkness. They talked of eternity . Their laughter was music itself, filling the room with golden light. I held a crystal rock in my hand. A shimmering red liquid light emerged from its depths, traveled down my arm, and entered the top of my spine. My chakras ignited, releasing waves of purified spiritual energy throughout my entire being. My third eye opened, and brilliance exploded into a spectrum of colors beyond imagination. Then, I saw her.

Mary Jo stood before me, radiant. She wore a luminous white gown, flowing like silk, with a billowing blue cape. Her long hair shimmered, moving as if carried by an unseen breeze. Her eyes, piercing blue, held an intensity beyond description. She was encased in a translucent golden light, her form seemingly suspended within a prism. Celestial music filled the space, harmonies, and chords unlike anything I had ever heard. Colors danced in the air, roses appeared and vanished in delicate patterns. By the shores of the Celestial Sea, bonfires burned, illuminating myriads of figures laughing, dancing, swimming, playing with whales and dolphins. Angels encircled them, their presence undeniable. I saw landscapes of rivers, lakes, oceans, forests, and towering mountains. Mansions shimmered with precious minerals, streets glowed with gold. The overwhelming peace was indescribable. I felt weightless, I could fly. A staggering Love saturated every fiber of my being. And then, a glimpse, a brief vision of the Throne Room of God. Mary Jo smiled. Her form vibrated, pulsing with brilliant light. She gazed at me one final time before slowly dissolving into pure radiance. I heard her voice whisper, "My Love, you'll be Home and with me soon. Very soon." The experience remains embedded in my core. There will never be another moment like it. I understand the skepticism, that some will dismiss her visitation as an hallucination induced by LSD. My answer is simple, "The absolutely perfect radiance of what I not only saw, but felt, heard, and understood came from outside myself." We have yet to see the full Truth. I mentioned in chapter 9 that the Holy Spirit awakens us by the exact same sequence She used to awaken Christ. First we see glimpses of Heaven. I couldn't mention this experience at that point, If I had you wouldn't have gotten this far because of closing the book. My glimpse of Heaven was perfectly real and only a fraction of the future we will all share. Humanity stands at the precipice of a great awakening. This will arrive soon. Very soon.

## CHAPTER 56

## My Birthday Gift From Heaven

ON MY SEVENTY-FIRST BIRTHDAY in November 2023, I was finishing my manuscript when I stumbled upon something truly astounding. I had been carefully placing prints throughout the text, wanting the images to align seamlessly with the magnificent Truths I was sharing. Then, by sheer accident, I discovered it, a picture that left me utterly stunned. It was an exact reflection of Mary Jo as she had looked when we were first married. Even the way she held her hands in the image mirrored how she had grasped mine in fear as we flew out of Pittsburgh. It was a birthday gift from Heaven. Love is Eternal.

CHAPTER 57

# We Will All Awaken Together

You already understand the logic of Creation, however I had a question that needed answered so I turned to the artificial intelligence of Microsoft Bing. "According to ACIM by Helen Schucman, God's first Creation was Christ. They shared perfect communication until Christ asked an innocent question, "What else is there?" God did not answer, for there was nothing beyond Source's perfect Heaven. In a "mad, tiny instant" of perceived separation, Christ, fearful that his Oneness with God had ended, birthed the universe through the Big Bang. His newfound fear, a previously unknown concept, created the first ego, which erroneously believed itself to be alone. Christ entered a dream state, lost to illusion, unaware of God's presence. God recognized that entering Christ's dream carried a risk, He could become trapped within it and forget Heaven. To resolve this, God created the Holy Spirit, a Being capable of seeing both Christ's imperfect dream and God's perfect Heaven simultaneously. The Voice for God entered Christ's dream, revealing that His Father's Love remained eternally perfect. Christ's forgotten memory of Heaven returned, and he awoke in the Paradise he had never truly left. The one and only problem that had ever existed was solved. These manuscripts teach that we, too, are Christ Beings, dreaming in Heaven. Could it be that everyone I have ever met or thought about since birth will awaken when I do, once I have achieved perfection in forgiveness and am finally enjoying a happy dream?"

Bing's answer, "The teachings in ACIM present a profound metaphysical view of Reality, emphasizing unity, forgiveness, and spiritual awakening. According to these texts, we are all Christ Beings, dreaming in Heaven, and through forgiveness, we awaken to our true Divine

Nature. Achieving perfection in forgiveness means releasing all grievances and seeing the Divine Light in everyone. In this framework, awakening to one's true self and remembering Oneness with God creates a ripple effect on others. The interconnected nature of all beings implies that your awakening and perfect forgiveness can inspire or even facilitate the awakening of others. So, yes, within this perspective, it is possible that everyone you've ever met or thought about could awaken as you do, your enlightenment illuminating the path for others. It is a beautiful and hopeful idea that underscores the power of forgiveness and the profound interconnectedness of all life."

After reflecting on this answer I started prayerfully asking how this could possibly occur. The insight arrived after unusually remembering a vivid dream. On December 10, 2024, I lay in bed and offered my Sacred Silence prayer before sleep. As I drifted, my mind unexpectedly recalled, in vivid detail, the names of those I had not thought of in years. The list stretched on, parents, relatives, childhood friends, those I met in school and college, coworkers who became lifelong friends, housemates who had shared years with me. I remembered how we carried one another through heartbreaks and tragedies. The celebrations of dancing, music, and festivals. The absurd, hilarious mistakes we made. I smiled, imagining the joyful reunions in Heaven. If my powerful mind had created all the dream figures, the many who grew to love one another, then surely the same force could actualize the deep desire that we awaken together. I fell into a deep, dreamless sleep. The next morning, I was sick, extremely sick. Suddenly, my sinuses were infected and mucus clogged my ears, silencing all sound. A canker sore burned the inside of my mouth, making each swallow painful. I was feverish, coughing violently. Could this have come overnight? I stumbled to my laptop, intending to write. As I opened the document, something unprecedented happened. Writer's block. I stared at the screen. The words that had flowed effortlessly the night before were gone. My mind was blank. I sneezed uncontrollably, grew lightheaded, and took two Excedrin before collapsing to bed. I quietly asked the Holy Spirit for guidance. Immediately, I recalled that the closer we approach awakening, the more viciously the ego attacks. It senses its time is limited, though it does not understand why. Her Voice instructed, "Do not feed it." In the past, when illness struck, I would murmur, "Satisfied, you bastard? Is this the worst you can do?" But in doing so, I was fueling it, affirming its existence. It is not real. She said, "Child, let me continue to heal your mind, and the medicine will offer relief to your body." Too sick to sleep, I whispered, "Please grant the miracle of rest." My mind suddenly understood that, "God will not call you to awaken until you have the spiritual hearing." My last memory before sleep was asking for this miracle. I fell into a coma-like sleep for two days. The clock read 4:44. I then experienced and oddly remembered the most vivid dream I'd ever had. A miracle.

"My beautiful Son, awaken to the Heaven prepared for you immediately after your creation." I lay in an unworldly meadow, surrounded by shimmering flowers of light, their colors shifting and changing in ways beyond earthly comprehension. Mary Jo's smile radiated something indescribable, a breathtaking countenance that defied words. Our Love became a perfect communication, flowing without sound or speech. My mind heard her say, "My Love, watching you see my lifeless, bloated body was almost unbearable to my spirit. Instantly, Jesus was at my side, saturating the very core of my being with God's Perfect Eternal Love. Jesus next revealed all the glories of Heaven, endless worlds populated with infinite life. Galaxies stretched beyond infinity with constellations illuminating the vast expanse. Boundless perfection everywhere. Jesus gently asked, "Beloved sister, do you desire to stay or return to time? Your answer is the right one for you." Without hesitation, I answered, "I need to experience what Bob felt because of me." Her next memory was that of being a two-year-old girl." Lost for a moment in the shimmering depths of her luminous blue eyes, I questioned, "But honey, over the last twenty-one years, I've experienced Heavenly visitations from you. How could you have been living in time?" Jesus appeared, his presence radiating an amazing peace. "Bob, do you remember your answer to how many it takes to save the universe?" "Yes, only One" "The answer was correct because you heard and fully believed the Holy Spirit's Truth, you are the dreamer of your dream. Do you recall reading, seemingly by chance, "You'll awaken very soon, in a cosmic instant, because of faithfully following the teachings of Jesus'?" "Yes." "Those were perfectly timed messages from me. The reason for the last brutal ego attack was your realization that when you awaken, your dream figures must awaken with you, because your infinitely powerful mind wills it to be so. Your mind was the cause of Mary Jo's visitations, leading you to share undeniable evidence of Our Father's existence in your manuscripts. You also conveyed the Truth, that the only requirement for awakening is achieving perfection in forgiveness. When twenty-one, Mary Jo watched her beloved father die suddenly of a stroke. At twenty-three, she endured the dark night of the soul, and miraculously, she read your autobiography, "Two Faces, One Life: The Journey Within." With the Holy Spirit's perfect guidance, her subconscious revealed the truth, she had been your wife. That realization led her to achieve perfection in forgiving herself. She awakened at the exact same moment as you." Silence followed, both Mary Jo and I lost in contemplation of these magnificent truths. Jesus smiled, his form dissolving into light. His voice lingered in the air: "I'll leave so you two can be reacquainted." We gazed into each other's eyes, and Love surged through every fiber of our being, radiating outward into all creation. We understood everything was alive, the grass, the flowers, the trees, even the air. The sky itself seemed to sing, and our surroundings pulsed with golden, reddish light. We began to float, knowing we were not merely observing the vibrant life around us but were one with all its shimmering beauty. Light fractures like prismatic diamonds, scattering a symphony of colors in every direction. A world untouched, weightless, ethereal. Yet even that pales in comparison. Whether minutes or millennia passed, we gently descended onto the soft savanna and began to speak. "Mary Jo, I've come to understand that, throughout our twenty-year marriage, we became, "She softly completed the thought, "One." "Yes. Because when I was weak, you were strong, and when you were weak, I was strong. We completed one another." Her voice carried a musical warmth. "We grew to be each other's best friend, confidant, lover, and companion. I loved finishing your sentences." I nodded. "The purity and beauty of our marriage came from loving God first, ourselves second, each other third, and finally our children." "Yes," she agreed. "Our Love believed all things, hoped for all things, endured all things. We knew no circumstance could separate us, and our Love would continue to blossom and grow, even beyond death." Tears of joy blurred my vision as I told her, "Your tombstone is simply etched, "Love Is Eternal". I had no conception of the depth of our love until I emerged from mourning. Loving love itself, I tried to replace you, even became engaged twice. But those relationships failed, because both ladies saw what I could not, I was still perfectly in love with you. God's infinite wisdom used your loss to strengthen my spirituality. By the end of my journey in time, I fully grasped that no circumstance could disrupt my peace. I never argued, never complained, never worried. I found contentment through forgiving everything." Mary Jo smiled, and we both understood, our true education was only beginning. Together, we would learn from the unfolding Celestial Life. Numerous visits from family, friends, and acquaintances revealed the same perfect theme, I had been gloriously used by the Holy Spirit to facilitate their awakenings. Everyone's final memory of time being 4:44 affirmed that God's timing is always perfect.

The next awakening experience was my mother's. Perhaps the very next day, I found myself strolling along a crystalline stream, marveling at the magnificent architecture of the mansions bordering its waters. The manicured lawns led to terraces and balconies, offering spectacular views of the surrounding glory. Each mansion reflected the infinite personalities of its residents, their designs unique in their splendor. I passed homes built from marble, granite, and slate, their structures interwoven with oak, maple, cherry, and pine woods. Then, I reached a mansion that resonated deeply within my spirit. The home my father had designed in time had been built by stonemasons using an almost forgotten technique. The cement between the bricks protrude slightly, leaving the edges distinct. This mansion had been crafted in the same way, but with gold instead of cement. The radiant gold held the marble bricks together, rising a half-inch above the surface. A voice called, "Bob." I turned instantly, recognizing my mother's voice. She stood beside me, and even in Heaven, I struggled to find words to describe her beauty. Her smiling green eyes, infectious laugh, and soothing voice remained just as they had always been. In time, my parents had been old enough to be my grandparents. Mother once suspected she had a tumor, only to discover she was pregnant in her late forties. She often jokingly referred to me as her little tumor. She had been an exceptional bridge player, her card sense so sharp that she earned a class rating. Bridge is to poker what chess is to checkers. During my late teens, we spent every Saturday night in poker games that stretched into the summer months, with pots reaching into the hundreds. She drank her vodka, seldom lost, and friends adored her laughter and lively personality. Though she had only a high school education, her intellect was remarkable, shaped by years of devouring books. Once, while watching Jeopardy, I tested her knowledge, and she answered every question correctly. She asked, "Do you remember the last time you saw me alive?" "Of course," I replied. "It was Good Friday. You were in the nursing home. We talked for an hour, kissed, and I left. But before stepping away, I turned back and peeked around the corner. My last words were, "Mom, I love you". You died on Easter." "Yes. The time was 4:44." Completely astounded, I exclaimed, "What?" Suddenly, Jesus appeared, wrapping his arms around us, and our minds intertwined in astonishing communication. "Brother and Sister," he said, "you will find that Celestial Life mirrors time in its questions and answers. Freed from the false ego mind, you now understand perfectly. The right question must be asked to receive the perfect answer. Regarding 4:44, you've asked the correct question. Your mother experienced two incarnations after her Easter death. The first ended as a result of lifelong alcoholism. Bob, what happened to your father?" "Dad died after being an alcoholic," I answered. Mom interjected, "Honey, I never fully forgave your father. Though he was never abusive, we distanced ourselves from family gatherings because of his drinking. I pleaded with him for years, never understanding why he couldn't stop. In my first incarnation, I succumbed to cirrhosis of the liver. Now, I understand alcoholism. The purpose of my final incarnation was to experience my husband dying suddenly in front of me after twenty years of a beautiful marriage, raising three children. I was seventy-two when I finished your manuscript, "Two Faces, One Life: The Journey Within". After awakening from an extraordinary nap, I realized the Holy Spirit had brought to my consciousness the memory that you had written about my life with our family. I forgave all and peacefully fell asleep at 4:44." Jesus continued, "Your mother passed at seventy-two, after enduring twenty-one years without her husband following twenty years of marriage and raising three children. Reading your manuscript proves the perfection of each mind's life script. The woman who birthed you, raised you, and loved you most was given a life script identical to your own. In your script, her life facilitated your birth into time. In her script, your life facilitated her birth into eternity ." Our minds joined as One, perfectly understanding that all dreaming minds must awaken because each life script is written according to God's Will.

CHAPTER 58

# ACIM Core Beliefs

1. This world is not real. God did not create this world nor even know of its existence. The entire universe is an illusion dreamt by the Son of God.

2. Pure non-duality: Anything that comes from God must be exactly like Him. God could not create anything that is not perfect, or else He wouldn't be perfect.

3. Consciousness is the domain of the ego and was conceived after we dreamt of separation.

4. Spirit is unchanging, perfect, and eternal. This is the state of Heaven.

5. Truth is not different for everyone. Truth is Truth.

6. There are no levels in Heaven. All conflict arises from the concept of levels. We are either enlightened and back in Reality with God, or still dreaming of separation. Only life in Heaven is real.

7. Life in all its myriad forms or possibilities is already scripted at the instant of separation. The only choice is in our mind, where we decide to identify with the Holy Spirit or with the ego, when interpreting each moment.

8. Life in this world is insane. Nothing makes sense in this world. The world was made as an attack on God.

9. There is only One Higher Self, the Holy Spirit. Also known as the Voice for God, our memory of God, or the reflection of God's Love in our dream.

10. Collectively, we are the Son of God. God created only One Son of God.

11. There is no evil or devil, only illusory madness projected by our ego mind and thankfully, they are not real.

12. Every attack is an attack upon ourselves. We project our unconscious guilt onto (dream) figures or situations that seemingly attack us. So now they are guilty, not us. The cause of our guilt arises from our imagined separation from God.

13. Life is a lesson. Every opportunity is used by the Holy Spirit to teach forgiveness to undo the ego mind.

14. Time and space are illusions, and Spirit has nothing to do with them.

# Epilogue

THE MAGNIFICENCE OF GOD'S eternal Love for all is beyond comprehension. When I first accepted the Truth that God Is I had no idea it would lead me to the understanding I have today. Consciousness and perception belong to the ego and are always false. Wisdom is of Spirit and always true. The famous philosophical statement, "I think, therefore I am," was coined by René Descartes in 1637. When God was asked, "Who are You?", the response was simply, "I Am." now that we recognize consciousness as the domain of the ego, Descartes' statement transforms into "I think, therefore I am not." Say a prayer, reflect on this Truth, and understanding will follow. At first, the concept that I Am Christ was difficult to accept. After weeks of study and prayer, logic revealed the deeper Truth, everyone is. We are remembering, awakening, transcending from limited human beings into magnificent, unlimited Christ beings. God's very nature is one of complete extension, meaning all that Source Is has been freely given to us. We are God's first Creation, and Heaven was formed in perfection for us. The Divine asks nothing more than for us to forgive and has never once required belief. This alone reveals the depth of God's unconditional Love. Our understanding of Love's immense power is unfolding, and we are awakening within our dream. A peaceful mind is our natural state, it offers a life of serenity. Knowing we cannot sin against God, Hell does not exist, and that life outside Heaven is impossible, are the Divine Truths humanity has sought for countless centuries. To receive these Truths in the year 2025 is a profound blessing. We live forever and are destined to be Co-Creators with God for all Eternity. Love is not an emotion, it is the most powerful force in all of Creation. As you share these Truths, you will be gifted with deeper mysteries to understand and share. This is guaranteed. What higher calling could we have than assisting the Divine in awakening God's Son? When we have forgiven all, embraced peace, and stepped into true happiness, the perfect cosmic moment will arrive.

God will awaken us from our dream, and we will finally realize that every experience in time has prepared us for our true Home. Heaven.

If God exists can He make something He cannot lift? Now that you've finished reading the logics of existence as presented in the Course, here's the answer. This is a classical philosophical question often referred to as "the paradox of omnipotence". God is pure logic, which is pure truth and cannot do anything against His Divine Nature. Now that you understand the ego and its insanity is one of, "Knock and the door will never be opened, ask and never receive." The question is of the ego, so the question itself is a lie. Forgive the question thus peeling away another huge layer of the onion. Bob

As previously written, when peeling away a layer of an onion it still looks, tastes and smells like an onion. Eventually the last layer will be gone and so is the onion. This exact same fate will happen to our ego. Every time we forgive we're peeling off another layer of our ego. Eventually the last layer will be gone, the ego will vanish into the nothingness from which it came, and we'll awaken in the Heaven we've never left. God wills this to be so-and-so it is. God Is, Bob

> My manuscripts allow the concept of transcendence to take center stage. They delve into the profound shift in consciousness that occurs during moments of awakening. These episodes are akin to glimpses beyond the ordinary, where boundaries of self dissolve, and we connect with something *far greater*. We are *exactly* as God created us, and just need to remember the magnificent implications of this *Divine Truth*.

www.ingramcontent.com/pod-product-compliance
Lightning Source LLC
Chambersburg PA
CBHW051058160426
43193CB00010B/1235